Rerouting . . .

Finding Our Way Back to God and His Church

Fr. John Riccardo

the WORD
among us®
press

Published by The Word Among Us Press
7115 Guilford Drive, Suite 100
Frederick, Maryland 21704
www.wau.org

22 21 20 19 18   1 2 3 4 5

ISBN: 978-1-59325-332-5
eISBN: 978-1-59325-507-7

Cover design by Faceout

Made and printed in the United States of America

Library of Congress Control Number: 2018936434

This book is dedicated to the people of God at
Our Lady of Good Counsel in Plymouth, Michigan.
More specifically, it is dedicated to
Fr. Prentice Tipton, Fr. John Simoneau, Fr. Pierre Ingram,
Deacon Dave Carignan, and Mary Delpup.
Rerouting, as it was originally conceived, was the fruit of
a tremendous amount of prayer, some wonderfully lively
discussions, more prayer, and hard work.
It is such a joy to serve the Lord with all of you!

Contents

Where Are We Going?

It's time to face reality, which means it's time to admit there's something missing in the religious experience of many Catholics these days. It's also time to admit that what's missing is not just important; it's vital and needs to be recovered. I suspect many Catholics are aware of missing something, even if they can't quite identify what it is. I suspect that this awareness is probably most intense during Mass on Sunday.

Why? Because every Catholic knows that the Mass is supposed to be the heart of our spiritual lives. The Mass is "the source and summit of the Christian life" (*Lumen Gentium*, 11). Is it really, though? How many Catholics would actually say that the Mass is the highlight of the week for them?

I know it wasn't for me many years ago. I knew something was going on up there, but I didn't get it. And now, as a priest, I know that the pews are full of people who are just as I once was. They can't quite perceive the spiritual reality that is present in the Eucharist, and they don't understand what gives vibrant life to the faith they profess in the Creed.

Without such an awareness, what eventually happens? People become spectators at the liturgy, bored onlookers at a bewildering ritual, rather than participants in a profound sacramental reality. That becomes frustrating—how could it not? Sometimes the frustration becomes so great that people start asking themselves questions like these: *What am I doing in church? Why did I even bother to come?*

These are sad, almost desperate questions. And they often pave the way for a kind of tragedy—in fact, for a triple tragedy. First, it's a tragedy for the individual, who might turn his back on the Church and thus may never know a deep and lasting relationship with Jesus. Second, it's a tragedy for the Church to lose a unique and valuable person with all his or her potential for holiness. And third, it's a tragedy for the world at large, which longs to hear the good news of what God has done for us all in Jesus, even if they don't know it. These tragedies occur—often unnoticed—every day in our Church, as people give up searching for that mysterious something they are missing and have never been equipped to find.

Finding our way

And that's the real problem. Most of us have never been taught how to find our way into the heart of our great religion, how to progress from spectator to deeply involved participant. To be a Catholic requires faith. There's no news there. But it also requires knowledge, and that's something we may not know—or at least may not have thought about very much. Here's an uncomfortable truth: although Catholic thought, from the Fathers of the Church to the most contemporary theologian, is too vast to be contained in the largest library this world has to offer, many Catholics are unaware of any of it. That's another tragedy.

The teachings of the Church are beautiful and inspiring. They can and will sustain us throughout our lives, just as they have sustained innumerable people before us. But they will not be able to do that if we don't understand them, at least in a basic way.

All the Church's teachings flow from the same source. One teaching builds on another, until they form a vast and consistent structure, a framework that is incredibly solid yet still very alive. It's like a huge tree with many branches, countless leaves, and roots that dig deep into the soil.

We need to understand something of that living structure and grasp the essence of that framework if we are to lead truly Catholic lives. Otherwise we risk seeing the Church's teachings as mere man-made rules that have no relationship to our lives or our contemporary world. And if that's what you believe, I ask you, how long will it be before you discard those rules?

I know it's a cliché to say that life is a journey, but it's still true. In fact, our earthly life from beginning to end is the only journey that matters, because it's the one that can take us to the Father and the eternal life Christ won for us. But don't think this is a journey in which we're carried along like a leaf in a stream of water. It's one in which we have to participate, plot a course, make sure we're on the right road and headed in the right direction. Each of us is in the driver's seat as we make our personal journey, and frankly, many of us are lost on the highway without the slightest clue as to which way to go.

And that's yet another tragedy, because the journey to God is unlike any other journey. It's the journey to that ultimate reality that gives meaning and value to everything that has meaning and value. If we are lost on our journey to God, we are lost, period.

How often do we hear people say things like: *Is this all there is? What's it really all about? Why am I here? Where am I going? How do I find lasting happiness?* Those are the questions that our God answers, but we can't hear the answers until we understand what our faith *is*.

Telling the story

Some time ago, when discussing this problem with my archbishop, I expressed a desire to do something a bit different during Mass in our parish. People repeatedly tell me that they just don't know the Bible very well. Without an understanding of "the story"—what we might call the "narrative arc"—it can be difficult to get anything out of the readings in the Liturgy of the Word. At most, people hope that the homily will help them make sense of what might seem unintelligible, include a joke, be relatable, and of course, not be too long. People may not even "get" what is happening on the altar during the Liturgy of the Eucharist. Is this what Mass is supposed to be?

With this in mind, I asked my archbishop, Archbishop Allen Vigneron, if I could try to create something we could do during Mass that would help people understand the story, the narrative arc. My hope was that if we could get the basics, the essentials, right, people could better understand the various excerpts from the Bible that we hear on any given Sunday as well as the sacrifice taking place at the altar. That proposal became what we called *Rerouting*.

In essence, *Rerouting* is a proclamation of what the Church calls the *kerygma*. *Kerygma* is a Greek word that refers to the proclamation of the life, death, and resurrection of Jesus. The first Christians—those who walked and ate with Jesus, who saw him heal lepers and the blind, who saw him raise Lazarus from the dead, who were there when he was crucified, who saw him in the flesh after he had risen from the dead, and who received the outpouring of the Holy Spirit on Pentecost—didn't proclaim the *kerygma* simply to give people some new information. They proclaimed Jesus so as to move their friends, family, and coworkers to respond. They did it because they were convinced that knowing Jesus is the best gift anyone can ever receive. They did it because they knew that encountering him was the best thing that ever happened in their lives.

And we who live today, who have encountered Jesus and have come to know him, do the same. We tell others about Jesus quite simply because we are convinced that he and he alone can show us what we are all so desperately searching for: happiness. He's the One who can lead us all home.

On the road home

Rerouting will put you on the right road and point you in the direction of that place where faith and understanding meet and flourish. Its aim is to steer you around the roadblocks that have been placed in your path by our secularized and shallow world and take you to your destination.

Think of being in your car on a trip to a place you've never visited before. Your GPS device is telling you when and where to turn. It guides you around traffic jams and roadwork; it warns you that the bridge further down the highway has been washed out and directs you to one that is still passable. That's rerouting in a worldly sense. Now it's time to turn off your device and try rerouting in a spiritual sense.

Many people, despite not clearly grasping why they should come to Mass, still do. Many people lacking a clear understanding of their faith still try to live it. In my mind, a major miracle takes place every Sunday at countless Catholic churches across the country and the world: despite so many not understanding the Mass, despite so many not having a profound friendship with Jesus, despite so many not believing in the real presence of Jesus in the Eucharist, people are *still* there! These are the people who yearn to be rerouted to Jesus. The yearning is in their hearts; only the direction is lacking.

So let's begin to be rerouted in the right direction, the one that will take us to our ultimate goal. Let's stop being mystified onlookers to our faith and become full and fulfilled participants. Let's open the door to that mysterious thing that's been missing, which—in case you haven't realized it— is nothing less than a life-changing encounter with Christ, the one who gives meaning to our lives and makes us complete.

1. On-Ramps

Getting on the Road Means First Discarding False Notions

What's an on-ramp for? To bring you to the road that will take you to your destination, of course. Maybe you were once on the right road but left it because you thought another route would be better or easier. Maybe you got lost and drifted from the right road without realizing it. But all that's over now: you're ready to reorient yourself and start heading in the right direction.

And that's easy when you're on an actual highway in a fast-moving car. It's more difficult when you're dealing with things deeper than direction and speed.

The on-ramp that brings us to real faith might be a little longer than we expect. That's because traveling on it means discarding old and erroneous ideas and replacing them with concepts that are not just true but capable of leading us to ultimate truth. Here's the goal as we travel these particular on-ramps, and it's very specific: to learn to see things as they are rather than as the world often thinks they are.

So let's begin.

First, we have to understand that we live in a culture that doesn't just *influence* what we think—it often *determines* the way we think. Sometimes it even dictates what is *possible* to think. Our secular culture's ideas about religion, and especially about Catholicism, are usually nothing short of toxic. Yet these ideas have been seeping into our minds for a long time—so long that we often don't even notice how foreign and damaging they are.

Materialism, the belief that there is nothing more than what meets the eye, is the default position for many. Relativism, the belief that values and morals are grounded in nothing more solid than emotion and personal preference, is taught on most college campuses and is the stuff of every sitcom we watch. Belief in God is considered a relic of the past—an irrational, unreasonable, and even bigoted relic. I could go on, but I don't think I have to. And I don't think I have to tell you that all these things add up to a problem, not just for our spiritual lives but for our entire Church. In fact, they add up to a kind of sickness.

We've all heard that the Church is a body, the mystical body of Christ. We comprise that body, you and I and countless others. Jesus is always the head, but we—frail and fallible as we are—remain the body. Like all living things, bodies can be invaded by pathogens and become ill. Sometimes those pathogens actually affect the DNA of the body they attack.

In a way, we're facing a change in the Church's DNA that results in mutations of important truths and doctrines. Profound religious ideas are flattened out; their holiness is drained away, drop by steady drop. Something that was once overflowing with significance becomes an empty shell.

In our culture—which is sometimes called post-Christian—this mutating process has run deep into the minds of Catholics, and it has affected our understanding of some fundamental concepts. Yet often we're unaware of these transformations, mistaking mutated forms for the real thing. When that happens, our spiritual lives become deformed.

We're going to examine some of the most significant secular-influenced mutations and contrast them with what the

Church really teaches. In other words, we're going to find the right on-ramps and follow them to their destination. Let's begin with a really basic concept, one that has undergone a particularly troubling mutation.

Faith

What word could be more basic to our understanding of our relationship to God? Yet what does it really mean?

If we listen to a new atheist like Richard Dawkins, we learn that faith is nothing more than belief without evidence. If we listen to someone who thinks in relativistic terms, we'll get a definition that is no better and may be worse: "Faith is just one of many possible interpretations of reality, a private belief in some invisible realities that have little or no bearing on how the world works or how you live your life. Faith has and should have no effect on the way you live your life."

Can you think of a definition of faith that is more anemic or pointless than that? I can't. It's a textbook example of how to empty something important of its vibrancy and meaning and leave it ready for the trash heap.

So what does the Church tell us faith is?

Here's a definition that I borrow from my colleague, Fr. Pierre Ingram: "Faith gives us access to the truth. Faith plugs us into God's understanding of reality. Faith is opening my being to a word that has the power to transform all aspects of my life. Faith puts my entire life at God's disposal." Or as Fr. Francis Martin once summed up, "Faith is God's work in me to which I respond."

What a difference! Here faith is dynamic, multifaceted, and multidimensional. It's also profoundly relational and transformational. Faith is not something private that we dream up on our own, and it's not something arbitrary. In fact, it's not rooted in us at all! It's rooted in God and God's work in us.

The definition I just gave you differs drastically from the ones the secular world prefers. In the secular world's mutation, faith is subjective, a personal choice based on . . . on what? On whatever we choose to base it on, apparently. It's disconnected from anything outside us. This kind of "faith" can have no knowledge of the object of faith—God. In the mutation of this word, faith is turned into wishful thinking, a house built on sand. No, it's even worse than that: it's a shot in the dark.

Notice something else: it's very lonely. The relational element of true faith is missing. The idea that God's presence can even have an effect in our lives isn't there. In the mutated idea of faith, each one of us is alone, hoping against hope for whatever might seem best to hope for.

And that's not a great place to be.

Let's look at yet another definition of faith. The *Catechism of the Catholic Church* teaches us that faith is "man's response to God, who reveals himself and gives himself to man, at the same time bringing man a superabundant light as he searches for the ultimate meaning of his life" (26).

Do you notice a theme? In Fr. Martin's definition, we learned that faith is "God's work in me to which I respond." The *Catechism* tells us that faith is "man's response to God." In both these definitions, faith is an answer to something that comes from outside us and beyond us.

I'm sure we've all heard the term "the gift of faith." Well, this is what it means. It's always God who freely initiates the relationship, to which we respond in faith. Faith is a human response but one made possible by the divine love and the divine will. God draws the response of faith from us—the response that brings us into ever-deeper communion with him. Faith transforms us, allowing us to live not for ourselves alone but for God and others.

In this sense, faith is a gift of love—one that includes God's self-disclosure to us. As the *Catechism* tells us, the gift of faith is meant to guide us to "the ultimate meaning" of our lives." And what can the ultimate meaning of our lives be but God himself?

So faith is the definitive on-ramp. It illuminates the path home, but it does more than that. It *becomes* the path home.

A gift demands a response. We can accept it, reject it, or ignore it. What is the proper response to God's gift of faith?

To answer that, let's remember our Blessed Mother—the most perfect example of faith we have—at the Annunciation. Mary has no idea what lies ahead when she hears the angel's confusing message. Yet she ponders that message and even asks a question about it, allowing God to work in her, perhaps allowing herself time to respond to God's invitation in perfect faith. "Behold, I am the handmaid of the Lord, let it be to me according to your word" (Luke 1:38), she then says, accepting the will of God with her whole being, entrusting herself totally to another. And that's what faith ultimately does for us. It allows us to act totally, to be truly "whole beings."

There are a hundred ways of describing how faith transforms us, and it doesn't matter which way we choose to express it. It only matters that we respond to God's gift of faith and let that gift do its work in us. Let it permeate your life in such a way that you can learn to trust as Mary did, as God is calling each of us to do.

Now let's turn to the mutation of another vitally important concept, one every bit as basic as faith.

Church

So tell me: What is the Church? I bet that many people would respond by pointing to a building with a steeple and a cross. In other words, the Church is considered to be identical to her places of worship. Others might say that the Church is an institution that was developed by people to give expression to their religious beliefs and feelings. They might tell you that the Church is a place we go to in order to find people who believe the same things that we do, who find meaning in the same religious symbols and rituals.

If you delved a little deeper regarding those symbols and rituals, you might hear that they are creations of earlier generations, things that historically have been meaningful but are not intrinsically meaningful. In other words, as man-made artifacts, they can be discarded and replaced by other man-made artifacts. You might hear that the Catholic Mass is really no different from a silent Quaker service or a loud and energetic Pentecostal one. Each gets worshippers in touch with "something greater than themselves."

Thus the Church's teachings can be true or false only in a subjective and personal sense: they're true if they work for you, but they can never make any ultimate demand on you.

The Church's only real function is to open up some feeling of transcendence in your mind. The Church in this sense becomes almost a work of religious art—beautiful perhaps, but not necessary.

You might like the Catholic or Episcopalian or Baptist approach, or you might not. If not, there's a different kind of church down the street or in the next town. You just keep trying one after another until you find the one that makes you feel the way you think church should make you feel. There are hundreds of churches and religious institutions of various kinds. Surely there's one for you out there somewhere.

I hope I don't have to tell you that the understanding of Church I've just described couldn't be more different from the way the Catholic Church has thought of herself since the days of the apostles. But before we discuss the Church's self-understanding, I want to point something out: the above definitions of Church have something in common with the mutation of the word *faith*, which we've already discussed. They are lonely.

A Church understood in the mutated sense can never tell us anything about the God it tries to worship. All it can do is tell us about our own religious feelings. A Church viewed in this way cannot reveal God to us in any terms except the most subjective. It's an ambiguous and closed system, and it locks us into our own minds.

The Church—as Catholicism has always conceived her, as she is—is a living body. We've already mentioned that the Church is the body of Christ. This understanding is very old and very apt. The Church is simultaneously spiritual and physical. It includes countless souls struggling on earth as they make their journey to God and countless souls who are beyond this world, whose journeys are complete or at least all but complete. And that's why we call it a *mystical* body: it's in the world yet transcends the world.

The Church can also be thought of as a convocation. That word means a community that is called together. Called together by whom? By God, of course. The same one who calls us into faith calls us out of our mundane lives into something greater, into a living body and a profound union with Jesus. Once we understand the Church to be the result of that call, we see once again that we are drawn out of our isolation into relationship.

In the very act of hearing someone call to us, that call becomes a tangible part of our lives, and we must respond to it. In hearing the call, we come to know something of the one who calls us. Some knowledge of God is now possible. We now have far more than the religious dreams and longings that are at the heart of the mutated understanding of Church. Now we can encounter the love that lies at the depth of reality—in other words, we can encounter Jesus.

Here's something very important: at the heart of the Church's belief lies the Incarnation. God takes on flesh; he becomes one of us, living and dying and giving himself for us. If this is what we believe, then the Catholic understanding of the Church is the only one that makes sense.

Try to imagine Jesus saying something like this on Ascension Thursday: "I was with you for over thirty years, but my work here is done, and I'm heading home to my Father. See you in a few thousand years at the Second Coming. Oh, . . . and by the way, you're pretty much on your own until then . . . except for the Scriptures. Most of them will be written in a few decades. Of course, I have to convert Saul of Tarsus first, but that's definitely high on my to-do list. So hang on."

Does that work for you? I bet it doesn't. Jesus entered our world not simply to withdraw from it again. His presence remains in a living body—not the body of one man but the mystical body that is the Church, a body with a divine origin and a divine dimension. That means the Incarnation is not just an historical fact but a present reality. That also illustrates why there is one Church rather than many: a body is an organic unity, not something that can be split apart and put together like a jigsaw puzzle.

The Church's sacraments are profound mysteries and bearers of grace. It is through the sacraments—especially the Eucharist—that Jesus' presence remains not just tangible but active in our world. The Church's sacraments are assurances that we're never on our own, that Jesus is always calling to us and giving himself to us.

The Church, in its unmutated understanding, simultaneously participates in the spiritual world and the physical one. It is the means by which Jesus becomes present for us. This has nothing to do with buildings or subjective truth. It has everything to do with *objective* truth and everything to do with the God who insists on meeting us in our world and our lives.

Let's look at another word that is closely related to what we've just been talking about.

Parish

The mutated understanding of the parish is something like this: the place I go to Mass; the church building along with the rectory and school; an administrative district. Some might even think of a parish as a club where people get together, hoping to have their spiritual needs met. This is a static and even trivial understanding of the parish.

Now let's take a look at the Greek root for *parish*. It's *paroikia,* which has a surprising meaning: "a sojourning." The first thing we notice about this word is that it is far from static. In fact, it implies almost constant movement. A parish is not a place at which people meet. It is the Church in a particular place at a particular time on its journey—its sojourn—to God. Perhaps we can even say it is the Church *incarnated* in a particular place at a particular time.

Let's recall the original biblical sojourner, Abraham. We meet him in the Book of Genesis, when God calls to him to leave his settled life and go to a distant land. Abraham does so with his wife, Sarah, slowly moving westward, trusting in the call of a mysterious and invisible (but active!) God. During their sojourn, Abraham and Sarah's life is marked by impermanence; tents taken down every morning and erected in a different place every night are their only home.

We're more like Abraham and Sarah than we'd like to admit. We might not journey from one land to another, but we journey—in fact, we hurtle—through our lives. We're in this world for only a brief period, and all our efforts to set down roots that will last forever are doomed to failure, because we live in a world that is not meant to last forever. Each microsecond moves us forward into a new present that then becomes the past; each microsecond increases the gulf between us and a past that can never be recaptured. We're all creatures of time, and there's no escaping that—which means that, like Abraham and Sarah's, our lives are marked by impermanence. We are constantly sojourning; we are constantly heading somewhere.

From her earliest days, the Church has understood this, and that's why she chose a word like *paroikia* to express the presence of the Church in various places. This understanding reminds us that as Christians, we don't make our pilgrimage alone but with others. It's a joint venture, a great company (remember that body that we were just discussing?) moving forward together. I pull my neighbor along when he needs it; he does the same for me.

So the unmutated meaning of a parish is that of the Church sojourning together in a particular time and place. Like Abraham and Sarah, we are constantly on the move in response to a call. Every day we reject the illusory permanence offered by the world as we move closer to what we have been promised: our only real home and a life that replaces transience with eternity.

Let's move on to our next term.

Laity

What is the mutated version of this word? For most of us, the laity simply consists of Catholics who have not been ordained to the priesthood or the diaconate and have not taken vows as members of a religious community. That's not incorrect, but it's incomplete.

In the hearts of many Catholics, the definition of *laity* might be more negative than that. They might say something like this: laypeople are the spectators of the Church, the ones who come to Mass and follow the rules. Someone might think along these lines: the laity is not intimately connected to the workings or mission of the Church, except as they might support them through the collection basket.

Inherent in all these ideas is the belief that laypeople have very few responsibilities as Catholics, that the mission of the Church is not their concern. Also inherent is the idea that laypeople are more like consumers than participants. They come to church to obtain certain services to which they are entitled.

Nothing could be further from the truth. To be a member of the laity is to be a member of the people of God—the people who have received and responded to the call from God that we have already spoken of. In the First Letter of St. Peter, there are these words about the laity: "But you are a chosen race, a royal priesthood, a holy nation, God's own people, that you may declare the wonderful deeds of him that called you out of darkness into his wonderful light" (2:9).

Here we see the dignity and grandeur that the laity is called to. The laity is called to nothing less than holiness, a holiness that is to be shared with the entire world.

What I am about to say will shock most people, so brace yourself: it's chiefly the laity's job to spread the gospel and transform the world. That's right; you're not supposed to be a passive onlooker—a consumer of something dispensed by the Church. You're certainly not supposed to sit in the bleachers, cheering your clergy team on as they confront the heathens. You're supposed to be a member of the team, an active evangelist. The ordained are to teach you, to shepherd you, to sanctify you with the sacraments, so that you will be able to go out into the world and transform it.

Think about it. If we want to bring Jesus to the wider world, who is better suited to the task than the people who are already in the wider world? Every structure of our society—the home, the workplace, the school, government, sports—needs to be evangelized. That can happen only if the laity, who is already in those structures, proclaims Jesus *within* those structures.

At the end of each Mass, the priest or deacon dismisses the laity using one of four possible formulations. Here are two of them: "Go and announce the gospel of the Lord," and "Go in peace, glorifying the Lord by your life." Those words exhort the laity to fulfill the vocation God gave them to spread Jesus's gospel throughout the world by their actions and words, by the lives they lead.

So there it is: the laity has an enormous responsibility. How many live up to it? How many are even aware of it?

I understand that the unmutated understanding of the laity is a daunting one. The temptation is to stick with the mutated version, which is much easier and very widespread. But if you want the Church to thrive, if you want Jesus to become known to more and more people, it's time to stop being a spectator and join the apostolate.

Do you know that word? Obviously it's based on the word *apostle*, and that means someone who is sent out to do something. The twelve apostles were sent out to bring the message of the kingdom of God to the entire world. That's still the Church's mission: to win the world to Jesus. An apostolate is any activity the Church engages in to fulfill this mission.

Who is called to participate in the apostolate? Everyone. As soon as we're baptized, we're called in this way. To participate in the apostolate is to become the Christian you were baptized to be.

In baptism, each and every one of us became a priest, prophet, and king. Before those of us who are priests were ordained, we were already priests, though of a different kind. Baptism makes each one of us share in the one unique priesthood of Jesus.

Now, priests do many things, but the simplest way to think of what priests do is this: they offer sacrifice. St. Paul, in his Letter to the Romans, urges us to offer ourselves as a living sacrifice to God (Romans 12:1). This task belongs to each one of us by virtue of our baptism. God gave me my life; he asks me to surrender it back to him with confident trust in his loving plan.

By baptism, we all share as well in the ministry of Jesus as the one prophet. Now, the word *prophet* conjures up lots of images in our minds. Perhaps we think of someone walking around saying, "Forty days, and Nineveh shall be overthrown," as Jonah did (3:4). And to be sure, prophets sometimes are called to do things like this. But a prophet is simply someone who speaks on God's behalf. This privilege belongs to all of us who have been baptized.

The culture around us often tries to tell us that faith is private, but the Scriptures couldn't be clearer: this is not true! God did not become a man and offer up his life so that only a few people would hear about it! We are all called to tell others about the one who not only loves but *is* Love.

And finally, in baptism we all are made to participate in Jesus' life as king. Now, kings, at least for many of us, are hard to relate to. My image of a king is that of someone who sits on a throne and is waited on day and night, often out of touch with the real needs of the people he is leading. But that's a mutated understanding of kingship.

According to a scriptural understanding, a king had three main tasks: to lead his army into battle (not merely to *send* them), to take care of widows and orphans, and to look after the poor. This is why the Church has always had a preferential option for the poor. We are to see with Jesus' eyes in order to look after those who are most vulnerable and to do all we can to care for their needs, even as the Lord does for us.

Now, all of this doesn't mean you have to wander the world preaching, baptizing, and risking martyrdom, as did the original Twelve. But it does mean that you can't be passive in the face of a secularizing and materialistic culture. Each of us must find a way to spread the gospel to those we encounter. Where do we start?

The answer is, you start where you are. Start in your family, really educating your children in their faith. Start by modeling that faith to them in every facet of your life. Work to become the Catholic you were baptized to be. That alone will have more effect than you can imagine, and it will eventually spill out of the confines of your family life into your professional life, your social life—every aspect of your world. Remember, your way may not be dramatic; it may even seem small and insignificant, as did that of St. Thérèse of Lisieux. But small things can be powerful, as Thérèse proved so well.

We've already discussed the Church as the mystical body of Christ. *The Decree on the Apostolate of Lay People*, which is one of the documents of the Second Vatican Council, uses that same understanding of the Church:

> In the organism of a living body no member plays a purely passive part, sharing in the life of the body it shares at the same time in its activity. The same is true for the Body of Christ, the Church; "the whole Body achieves full growth in dependence on the full functioning of each part" (Ephesians 4:16). (2)

So being part of the body of Christ means participating in its mission. The same document goes on to offer us these challenging words:

> Between the members of this body there exists, further, such a unity and solidarity (cf. Ephesians 4:16) that a member who does not work at the growth of the body to the extent of his possibilities must be considered useless to the Church and to himself. (2)

There you have it: some very hard words about the responsibilities of the laity. As you can see, there's just no way out of this one.

Are you ready to go on? Good, because the next mutation is something we all have to get straight.

Conversion

I'm pretty sure I know what you're thinking: conversion is something for other people. It's for non-Catholics coming into the Church, for atheists who have seen the light, for the major sinners we see on the nightly news. Conversion is a process people on the outside go through to enter the Church, to join the club.

Well, that's a good definition of the mutated version of the word. The real thing includes all that, but it is much more expansive and deeper. It's also more difficult. And it applies to every single one of us—even you and me.

Here are some difficult words: the goal of conversion is to live for another—for God. Yes, I know: that seems really unappealing, because to live for another seems somehow to lose ourselves, to give up our individuality, to become nothing, and that's the greatest human fear. So when St. Paul describes his own "living for another," there's something in his words that seems almost terrifying:

I have been crucified with Christ; it is no longer I who live, but Christ who lives in me; and the life I now live in the flesh I live by faith in the Son of God, who loved me and gave himself for me. (Galatians 2:20)

Who among us wants to say, "It is no longer I who live"? Not many, I suspect. Yet St. Paul does, and he seems joyful. Why? Because the one for whom Paul has decided to live is the one "who loved me and gave himself for me."

Would anyone give himself for me only to diminish me or even obliterate me? Of course not! Whom can I trust more to enhance my life than one who actually sacrificed himself out of love for my life?

So we see that this self-giving, which looks so suspiciously like self-eradication, is nothing of the kind. St. Paul shows us that it's really the doorway into a new and better way of living. He writes, "Therefore, if any one is in Christ, he is a new creation; the old has passed away, behold, the new has come" (2 Corinthians 5:17).

In living for Jesus, we are far from diminished. We become new creations, which means we become what we should have been all along. That's living for God, and that's the goal of conversion: letting the one for whom we decide to live transform us.

Now, most of us are not like St. Paul, and we're not likely to be knocked to the ground on the road to Damascus (or anywhere else) by a blinding vision of the risen Christ. So our conversion isn't going to be kick-started into the fast lane in one earth-shattering moment. Most of us are plodders; I know I am. We commit ourselves to Jesus over and over again and then fail to live up to that commitment over and over again. That's just the way it is with our frail humanity.

And that's also the way it is with conversion; it's a process that isn't complete until our earthly lives are complete. The point is to continue to commit and recommit, working with Christ as he works in us. Conversion in the unmutated understanding is the work of a lifetime, a lifetime in which we struggle toward that "new creation."

Conversion in its healthy, unmutated sense is never easy and can be very difficult, but it's a joy-filled process. Once we have entered the on-ramp of genuine conversion, we're really on our way to our destination. Who knows? With the help of Jesus, our conversion might even progress to a point where we can say with St. Paul, "It is no longer I who live, but Christ who lives in me." And if we reach that moment, we have arrived at human life at its fullest, meaning we have arrived at happiness. And who doesn't want that?

Now let's examine one last mutation.

Missionary disciple

I imagine that you're taking a look at this mutated term and breathing a sigh of relief. *I'm off the hook*, you might think. *Sure, I'm a disciple, but I'm no missionary. I'm just a normal person with a job and a family. In fact, I hardly ever leave the country, let alone go to mission territories.*

Those who have paid careful attention to the preceding sections, however, might be a little worried by now, for they're probably suspecting that *missionary* could have a deeper meaning than they've always thought—one that might even have something to do with them. Well, they're right.

The mutated idea of the word *missionary* is that it describes a religious specialty, almost a particular profession. Many people would describe a missionary as someone who is trained in specific techniques to go out into the world and convert people to the Church. Others might say a missionary is someone who travels to foreign lands and devotes his life to helping the poor and unfortunate while teaching them about Jesus. Throughout the history of the Church, there have been many brave men and women who have been so on fire with the love of Jesus that they did exactly that. They have accomplished enormous good over many centuries. Yet they are far from the only missionaries the Church has produced.

Let's recall for a moment our discussion of the true vocation of the laity. We learned that it is really the laity's duty to bring an awareness of Jesus to the world. Laypeople are primarily responsible for spreading the gospel, and they do that principally through the way they live in the world.

Isn't that a description of people engaged in missionary work? Yes, it is, and the fact of the matter is that to be a Christian is to be a missionary. It's that simple. Mission is a task entrusted to each one of Christ's disciples—ordained, religious, and lay. Each one of us participates not just in the mission of the Church but in the mission that *is* the Church, for the Church exists in the world to bring the world to Christ and therefore into right relationship with God.

In the final stirring words of the Gospel of St. Matthew, immediately before the ascension, Jesus presents to the Church her task in the world:

> All authority in heaven and on earth has been given to me. Go therefore and make disciples of all nations, baptizing them in the name of the Father and of the Son and of the Holy Spirit, teaching them to observe all that I have commanded you; and lo, I am with you always, to the close of the age. (28:18-20)

To be a Christian and a missionary is to take the central words of that quotation to heart. "Make disciples of all nations," Jesus tells us. If we are serious about out conversion, this command should come as a challenge but not a burden. If we are being transformed by Jesus, the desire to share what we are experiencing should rise within us and flow naturally to others.

"Go," Jesus told his disciples, and they did. They went into the entire known world, bringing the faith to whole nations and peoples. We too must go—but probably not so far. Most of us must simply go out into our own lives, the lives we share with others: into our workplaces, our schools, our business dealings, and our social relationships. In those settings, we can become subtle but powerful missionaries.

In the ancient world, many people were drawn to Christianity simply because the lives of the Christians around them were marked by a kind of peace and joy and hope that the world simply cannot give. Those early converts wanted to discover what the Christians had already found. People haven't changed much in two thousand years. Think how many people in our troubled world today are searching for the same kind of peace and joy and hope. Think what you have to share with them. And think what an act of love it would be to share knowledge of the only possible source of lasting joy and real salvation with such people. The simple truth is this: at the end of the day, it's either God and his love, or it's nothing at all.

How can we say we love Jesus if we don't try to bring him to those who don't know him? The essence of the healthy and unmutated version of a missionary disciple is simple. It is a Christian who loves Jesus and others and who yearns to bring him to those he encounters.

Does that describe you? If it's not, we've got some work to do.

So now we've examined six key Catholic ideas that have been mutated by our secular culture and compared them with the authentic concepts. Perhaps you didn't need this chapter because you knew this information already. Or perhaps your eyes were opened by it and you realized that your understanding of the faith was not what you thought it was. No matter what you thought of this chapter, you must never forget that we live in a culture that not only doesn't understand our faith but sees the entire world in a way that is very different from the way the Church does.

These six ideas are not the only ones that have undergone mutation. There are many more, and that fact makes it important for us to learn authentic Catholic teaching. It's not that hard; good materials are available in Catholic bookstores and probably through your parish. The important thing to remember is that Catholics cannot be passive in regard to our faith. We must be active, searching for proper information and learning to distinguish the Church's truth from the confusion our culture loves so much. That's the only way we'll be able to transform dead ends into on-ramps and get ourselves on the right road, the road that takes us to Jesus and eternal life.

Questions for Reflection and Discussion

1. What is faith? Why is it not true to say that "faith is blind"?

2. How is faith relational? How is it transformational? Why does it require a response from you?

3. Why is it important to understand the Church through the lens of the Incarnation? How does that affect your understanding of the sacraments? Of the fact that there can only be one Church?

4. How does your parish resemble a sojourn or pilgrimage? In what ways do you see people in your parish traveling together and helping one another along the way?

5. Why is it important to continue recommitting your life to Jesus? What happens if you fail to do this?

6. Would you characterize yourself as a "missionary disciple"? Why or why not? How can you grow in your desire to share the gospel?

2. Road Work Ahead

Slowing Down to Consider Why God Created Us

All our preparations are complete, we're on the road, and now we're traveling straight to the heart of the matter. In this chapter and the three that will follow, we're going to tell the entire story of the creation, fall, and redemption—or big bang one, big thud, and big bang two, as the philosopher Peter Kreeft puts it. That may seem like quite a tall order, but not only can it be done, we're going to do it. So it's definitely time to pay full attention while we take a close look at the opening chapters of the Book of Genesis—some of the most significant texts in Holy Scripture.

In fact, they're so important that I would say this: if you get these few initial chapters of Genesis right, you're well on the road to getting the entire story right. Sadly, that also means that if you get them wrong—as many people do—you're pretty much guaranteed to get the entire story wrong.

The Book of Genesis gives us two back-to-back creation stories. We're going to examine the first one here, and in the next chapter we'll examine the second one. Yes, that's right: there are two such stories, and they differ in many ways. What are we to make of that fact?

Let me answer that question very clearly: when there are two stories explaining the same thing in the Bible and they're in consecutive chapters, Scripture is telling you not to read those stories literally. They have to be approached differently from the way we approach history or biography. That doesn't mean that such stories aren't speaking truth. It simply means that the truth they contain is not scientific truth.

I think the best way of looking at this is to consider these writings inspired poetry. Poetry can reveal many deep truths, but those truths are different from the kind of truth obtained by scientific experiments or mathematical calculations. The point of such stories and the truths they contain is not merely to acquire new information or new data. The point is deeper than that. It's to encounter the Lord in his word and, in the process, to be filled with hope and with trust. This is especially true for the many among us who are anxious, fearful, and lacking a sense of meaning.

Now that we've established that, we're going to establish our goal for this chapter, which is to answer three crucial questions:

- Why is there something rather than nothing?
- Why did God make humanity? (In other words, why do you and I exist at all?)
- What does it mean to say that each of us is made in the image and likeness of God?

So let's begin with our first question—the most basic question that can ever be asked.

Why is there something rather than nothing?

The answer to that is really the whole point of the first chapter of Genesis. God is trying to reveal to us through this text why he created everything that exists. But if we're going to understand what God is telling us, we must be careful to keep exactly the right question in mind.

The question is *why*, not *how*. The Bible is not interested in asking how the universe was created. Science might answer that question eventually, and it will be a wonderful day if it does so. But as valuable as science is and as crucial and respected as it is by the Church, it cannot offer an answer to the most important question we can ask. It can never tell us why, only how.

Genesis does tell us why. It answers our question with a story, one I've already called a creation story. If you're in college or once were in college and studied ancient civilizations, you may be familiar with the term. Almost all ancient cultures had some kind of creation story, and more often than not, we are told that the biblical story does not differ in substantial ways from most of the others, that all these tales contain more or less the same basic elements. I have only one response to that assertion: rubbish!

Here's the truth: no matter the minor similarities, there is nothing in any of the ancient Near Eastern creation myths that resembles Genesis. The Near Eastern creation stories are graphic, often violent, and often highly sexual. They are certainly not the sort of thing you can read to your children, and if you ever tried to do so, you'd be beet red and tongue-tied before you had gotten very far.

The first and most obvious difference is that in most creation stories, there is not one God but many gods at work, and these gods often compete with each other. The second difference is that none of these gods is ultimate in power. Even taken all together, they are not in complete control but are subject to forces beyond themselves. Sometimes these forces are called the Fates or simply Fate.

The third difference is that these pagan gods are not good. In fact, they are often violent, avaricious, frivolous, lustful, selfish, and extremely unpredictable, all of which makes them seem more human than divine. Fourth—and probably most important—they make man to be their slave so that they can rest and play, which means that not only do they act more human than divine but they act like lazy humans. The fifth difference is that women in these stories are in no way equal to men. In fact, they have only one primary purpose: childbearing.

If the world is conceived of in this way, can the human being have any ultimate point, meaning, or destiny? No, of course not. If you believe the universe is created and conditioned by gods like the ones we've just described—arbitrary, selfish, and cruel—what worldview would dominate your thinking? I believe it would have to be one of despair—despair accompanied by anxiety and fear.

What could life in a world like that—a world without any ultimate meaning—possibly be about but the relentless pursuit of pleasure, power, and wealth? These are the sorts of things that might make you feel better for a little while, but they will ultimately fail or be taken away from you. We are describing a worldview in which there can be no lasting happiness—in other words, a worldview that can lead only to despair.

Does any of that sound familiar? I'm willing to bet that it sounds a little too familiar to most of us. Why? Because it's disturbingly similar to the worldview of the dominant culture in which you and I live. When you don't understand your origins and the goal of your life—where you come from and where you're going—and if you believe there's either nobody in charge or the one in charge can't be trusted to be good, then fear and despair must eventually reign. That's where the creation stories of basically all pagan cultures leave us, and I think we can all agree that's not a great place to be.

In contrast to that, let's look at the creation story in Genesis, which means we're turning to the very first verse of the Bible: "In the beginning God created the heavens and the earth" (1:1). These words are so famous that most of us know them by heart. In fact, they're so familiar that we probably don't even see how unusual they are. Well, let me give you a hint as to how unusual they are: there's absolutely nothing like them in any other creation story in the history of the world.

In this verse, we see right away that only one God is involved in the work of creation—not many, not several, not even two. That's my first point. Second, creation here has nothing to do with the killing of something or the birth of something, which means that this God doesn't create through some cosmic battle or in some sexual way.

Point number three is that this God is good. We could spend years searching the opening paragraphs of Genesis for some evidence that God is violent or lustful or avaricious or unpredictable, but we would fail. He is different from the gods of the surrounding cultures, not just in the fact that he is not one among many but in the fact that he really is good. Later we'll see that he's so good that he actually *is* love— not merely lov*ing* but Love. And that's another unique idea.

There is absolutely no evidence that any other ancient culture, especially in the Near East, ever thought anything like that about its deities.

Point number four is that the God of the Bible creates the universe out of nothing. The Hebrew word that we translate as "created" in the first line of Genesis is *bara*, and it implies a very special kind of creation, one limited to God. It is creation not out of preexisting materials but out of nothing at all.

In the biblical story, God is not a divine architect or construction worker. He doesn't build anything or tear anything down. He simply creates, and that brings us to the next point, which is that the God of the Bible creates not just out of nothing but effortlessly. We noted that the pagan gods were limited in their power. The way the God of the Bible creates shows he is supreme over all. Notice that there is no struggle in his work of creation. In fact, he has absolutely no interaction with any other entity. He doesn't try and fail and then try again. He doesn't create through some mighty and exhausting effort. He simply speaks, and things come into being—that's it.

Another contrast is that all the things the God of the Bible creates are good, and as we'll see, some of them are very good. He creates a world that is not based on conflict but is in harmony with itself and with him.

The next point is very important: the God of the Bible didn't need to make anything at all. He doesn't need creation in any way. He doesn't need man as a slave or even a companion. He is perfectly complete on his own. He creates only to fulfill his own will.

So using all that material, let's answer our first question: Why is there something rather than nothing? Why does creation exist? The answer is simple: because the good God willed to create it. That's why there's a universe. That's why there's anything at all. That's why there's a you and a me. The good God willed you and me and everything else into being out of nothing.

So now let's turn to our second question.

Why did God create humanity?

Remember that the pagan neighbors of the ancient Hebrews believed that their gods had created humanity to be their slaves. In simple terms, the gods created people so that their own lives could be easier—not a very appealing reason if you happen to be one of those people. The biblical view on the reason for humanity's creation couldn't be more different. To discover what it is, we'll take a look at the sixth day of creation:

> And God said, "Let the earth bring forth living creatures according to their kinds: cattle and creeping things and beasts of the earth according to their kinds." And it was so. And God made the beasts of the earth according to their kinds and the cattle according to their kinds, and everything that creeps upon the ground according to its kind. And God saw that it was good. (Genesis 1:24-25)

Notice the last sentence: "And God saw that it was good." These words are repeated over and over in the biblical creation story. Every time God creates something new, that line appears. So we can be certain that the Bible doesn't want us to miss it. Instead, it wants to drive the point home over and over again that everything God creates is good. Absolutely everything! The "beasts of the earth" and even "creeping things"—the things we go to great effort to avoid—are all good, at least at the moment of their creation. Why are they good? Because they are made by the one good God.

Now let's look at the verses that pertain to the creation of man. Be prepared to find in them something that is absolutely singular, something that is not even hinted at in any other creation story that has ever existed:

> Then God said, "Let us make man in our image, after our likeness; and let them have dominion over the fish of the sea, and over the birds of the air, and over the cattle, and over all the earth, and over every creeping thing that creeps upon the earth." (Genesis 1:26)

And there it is. The God of the Bible creates man not just as another animal and certainly not as a slave but as a unique being who somehow bears the divine image. The account of creation up to this point has been a kind of blow-by-blow or step-by-step description. But that changes now, because something new is happening: a creation that directly reflects the Creator himself is about to appear. When I read the above verse, I get the sense that God pauses for a moment. It is as if he enters into himself at this point to bring into being this special and final creation, a creation that is the culmination of all the work that God has been doing.

We're in search of an answer to our question: Why did God make humanity? Why did he make *us*? And that answer is most clearly expressed in the New Testament, in the Second Letter of St. Peter: the creatures who are made in the "image" and "likeness" of God are to be even more than that. We are to "become partakers of the divine nature" (2 Peter 1:4). The Eastern Church uses a special term for this: divinization. You were made for one purpose really, to be divinized.

Try your best to grasp as fully as you can the amazing fact that you and I and every single person in our troubled world was really made not simply to be a friend of God but to share in God's own life, his own happiness, his own joy, his own love, his own freedom, his own perfection for all eternity. That's the reason God made you. It's the reason each and every one of us exists.

When we've become aware of the overwhelming nature of our Father's plan for us, we can see signs of that plan in the biblical texts. The passage in which God creates man in his image ends with this simple declaration: "And there was evening and there was morning, a sixth day" (Genesis 1:31). So God chooses to make the one creature who bears his image and likeness on the sixth day of creation—the sixth day of the first week.

What is the sixth day in any week? It's Friday, of course, and that's important. Why? Jesus suffers and dies on a cross on a Friday. That means that man was created by God on a Friday, and when he was nearly lost to sin and death, man was recreated by God on a Friday.

Here's another sign: in the early chapters of Genesis, we see that the first man and woman are created by God and placed by him in a garden—the Garden of Eden. When Jesus nears the end of his earthly life, full of awareness of the horror he is soon to endure, what does he do? He goes to a specific place to pray to his Father—the Garden of Gethsemane. And when his passion—his re-creation of humanity—is finally over, he is laid to rest in yet another garden.

Do you think these things are coincidences? No biblical scholar does. Like any good piece of narrative literature, the Bible makes use of foreshadowing to help reveal the deeper meanings hidden in the story. These biblical facts are there to remind us that God has not and will never abandon his plan to divinize the ones he made in his image. He will go to any length to share his life with us.

You could spend your lifetime searching for these biblical connections and meditating on their meanings. But let's go on to our third question.

What does it mean to say that we are each made in the image and likeness of God?

The answer to this question is of massive importance to us. We don't have any hope of understanding who we are, what our place in creation is, or how we relate to God if we don't get this one right.

One way to get it wrong is to think that being made in the image and likeness of God has some physical dimension to it. In other words, that we must look something like God. We don't. We couldn't possibly, because God is pure spirit.

Nothing else in all of material creation has been made in God's image. We are alone in this respect. That gives us our first clue as to what it means to bear the divine image, the first of eight different but related points that we'll now consider:

- To be made in the image and likeness of God means that out of all creation, it is only you and I who are able to represent God on the earth.
- It means that we need to know who God is in order to live as we have been created to live. Knowledge of the One in whose image we are made is the only true road to knowledge of ourselves. But how do we acquire the knowledge of God that we need so desperately? Through Jesus, who is simultaneously God and perfect man.
- It means that we are commissioned by God to exercise dominion over the earth. Notice the word that I've used here. Dominion is not the same as domination. We are supposed to care for creation, not simply use it for our own purposes. That's why ecology is such an important concern of the Church.
- It means that we have an intellect and the capacity for reason; we can understand the order of things. We want to know the world around us, to comprehend it as deeply as possible.
- It means that we have been created with free will. We are not dominated by instinct, not simply swept along by events. But be careful. In a culture like ours, which has lost its way and certainly its understanding of God, we can confuse freedom with the ability to do whatever we want. That's lawlessness, not freedom. The *Catechism* tells us, "The more one does what is good, the freer one becomes" (1733). It also tells us that human freedom "attains its perfection when directed toward God, our beatitude" (1731). So our human freedom is not the unrestricted power to act on whim. It must be oriented toward the God who made

us free—the God who is goodness itself, reality itself. The ultimate purpose of our freedom is to love—to reflect God's love for us back to him. Only a being who is truly free can truly love. And God has made us for love because he's made us for happiness. Our freedom comes with responsibility. It gives meaning to our acts and decisions.

- It means that by use of our God-given reason, we can recognize God's voice urging us to do good and to avoid evil. The usual term for this is conscience.

- It means that you and I are ordered to God. St. Augustine put this very clearly and very beautifully when he wrote, "You have made us for yourself, O Lord, and our hearts are restless until they rest in you." Our culture strenuously rejects the fact that the human person is essentially religious. But faith is not an add-on or an option. You and I were literally made for a relationship with God, and we cannot be happy until we are in such a relationship.

- It means that we are created in a very specific way. Let's take a quick look at Genesis 1:27: "So God created man in his own image, in the image of God he created him; male and female he created them." This verse has tremendous significance. It means (among many other things) that the full reflection of the divine image isn't found in any one of us, that only man and woman together can fully reflect God's image. Man cannot exhaust what it means to be in the image of God, nor can woman. Sexual differentiation is essential to us, and it is a good thing. In fact, it's not just good; it's very good.

So there they are: eight elements that, taken together, should give us a good idea of what it truly means to be created in the image and likeness of God. As we think about them, they should make us aware of the awesome love with which our Father made us, the care he poured into his human creation. We should become more conscious of how special we really are in God's eyes and how unique is our role in his plan of creation. We should be not just grateful but humble, because we are all painfully aware that we are the creatures who fail God—who reject him—time and time again.

God's plan for his creation

Let's look at the rest of this creation story to find some clues as to what God has in mind for us, the pinnacle of his creation. In Genesis 1, we read:

> And God blessed them, and God said to them, "Be fruitful and multiply, and fill the earth and subdue it; and have dominion over the fish of the sea and over the birds of the air and over every living thing that moves upon the earth." And God said, "Behold, I have given you every plant yielding seed which is upon the face of all the earth, and every tree with seed in its fruit; you shall have them for food." (1:28-29)

The fact that God tells us what to eat and then gives us our food reminds us of two very important facts. The first is that we are contingent, dependent creatures. To be a creature is to have needs, to be vulnerable. But the second fact is that God will provide for our needs—not always our wants but our needs—like the good Father he is.

Notice in the above verse that at this point in the creation story, which is before the fall, nothing dies: no creature is killed to provide sustenance for another creature. Food for both man and the animals consists entirely of plants. The point is not to say that we should all be vegetarians. It's far deeper. It's that death is not part of God's original plan. Death is something that came later. In a couple of chapters, we'll see that death comes into our lives through our own doing.

We've come to the end of the first chapter of the Book of Genesis but not to the end of the first creation story. The seventh day of creation is still to come:

> Thus the heavens and the earth were finished, and all the host of them. And on the seventh day God finished his work which he had done, and he rested on the seventh day from all the work which he had done. So God blessed the seventh day and hallowed it, because on it God rested from all his work which he had done in creation. (Genesis 2:1-3)

These verses add something new. They introduce the Sabbath and highlight its importance. God rests on this day, and that is meant to show us that rest—ceasing from doing—not only is important but can actually be holy. Be sure to note that the Sabbath is presented here almost as a part of creation itself. It is what God "does" on the seventh day. So the Sabbath can be understood not as an afterthought or an add-on but as intrinsic to creation or even its culmination.

This is important. The Sabbath is meant to be a regularly recurring moment in our lives, during which we have the opportunity to step back and see things in a different light—through the lens of eternity. The *Catechism* tells us this: "The sabbath brings everyday work to a halt and provides a respite. It is a day of protest against the servitude of work and the worship of money" (2172). The Sabbath should give us at least a glimpse of what we were created to be: beings not completely devoted to toil and worldly activity but able to rest and focus on their relationship with their Creator and with each other.

Or at least that's the idea. But how often do we see this idea lived out in our culture or even in our own lives? One recent movie called Sunday "a day of the week that is owned by the NFL." There's enough truth in that to make us uncomfortable.

But God himself rests on the Sabbath. Perhaps we can even imagine it this way: God plays on the Sabbath. He loves to play. And you and I are created in his image in order to enter into his rest—to play, to give thanks, to worship, to enjoy.

Sunday is not a day to do nothing, and it is certainly not a day like any other day. It's a day when we should rest and play. So begin to observe the Sabbath: rest on Sunday; play with your kids; do the things you most love to do. But above all, remember the Lord, and thank him for giving you all that you have and making you all that you are.

One last thing regarding the Sabbath: What day does it fall on in the creation account? It falls on Saturday. God rests on Saturday. Now ask yourself if there's another Saturday during which God rests in Scripture. I probably don't have to tell you that it's Holy Saturday, the day on which the One through whom all of creation was made rests in a tomb. He rises the next day—Sunday—to go about his work of recreating the world that man has broken, of restoring the one creature who means most to him to a right relationship with God. And that, in case you didn't know it, is the reason the Church celebrates the Sabbath on the first day of the week rather than on the last.

Let's recap what we've said in this chapter in the simplest of terms:

- There's one God.
- He's good.
- He created everything.
- He did it out of nothing.
- He did it freely.
- He did it effortlessly.
- Everything he created was created because he loves.
- Everything he created was (originally) good.
- The highlight of everything he created was you.
- You were made in his image and likeness, and together man and woman fully reflect his image.
- God has a plan for his creation.

Every item on this list is vital, but the most important things of all are the ones that refer to God's love. Remember, when we started this journey, we asked three questions: *Why am I here? Where am I going? How do I get there?* The answer to every one of those questions—the answer to every meaningful question about our lives—is the same. It's love.

You are here because God in his love chose to bring you into existence. You are going to share in his own love and partake in his divine nature for all eternity. You get there through his love for you and through your love for him and for your neighbor.

We become aware of these things through reading Scripture. To know Scripture is to be healed. God's word not only shows us who we really are and where we're going; it can heal us of fear, of the fear that we're on our own in an indifferent or even hostile universe and that there is no ultimate point to life or to anything else.

But we know that there is a God, and God is a Father—a good and generous and loving Father. And we are not nothing; we are his beloved sons and daughters who are so loved as to be made in his image and likeness. Not only did this God and Father create us out of love, but he came to save us when we were lost. And not only that, but he loves us so intensely that he will repair the ruins we make of our lives day after day. And eventually, when our days on earth are done, he will draw us to himself, making us partakers in his own life.

And that's what we depend on. That's what gives us hope. That's what gives us joy.

Questions for Reflection and Discussion

1. Why did God create everything that exists? How does that change your worldview? How does it affect how you see and treat others?

2. What do you think it means to "become partakers in the divine nature" (2 Peter 1:4)? What might this look like in someone's life? In your life?

3. What does it mean to you, personally, to be made in the image and likeness of God? Which of the eight elements listed resonates most with you?

3. How do you spend your Sundays? What are some ways you can more deeply honor the sabbath rest God intends for you?

5. To know Scripture is to be healed. How has this played out in your life? How can the Scriptures help you understand God's desires for you? For the Church and the world?

3. Merge

Speeding Along, We Need to Discover
What Makes Us Happy

We're still speeding along, and we're eager to continue our journey because we've learned something important about ourselves: we are unique in creation—made in the image and likeness of our Creator. We've also learned that the God who made us and loves us beyond measure offers us incredible hope—a salvation beyond our dreams that actually includes a sharing in his own life.

Yet while we are well aware that God has made us for great things, we must still deal with our own rebelliousness and sinfulness. How does such a contradictory creature as man find happiness? Is it even possible to do so? That's what we'll explore in this chapter.

So let's begin with an unusual question: Who doesn't want to be happy? Or maybe we should ask that in a slightly different way: Who among us wants to lead a miserable, banal, unfulfilling life?

Are you thinking long and hard to come up with an answer? Probably not, because the answer couldn't be more obvious: no one desires to be unhappy. We all understand on a very basic level that it's simply part of being human to want to be happy. Different people might have very different and even contradictory ideas of what will bring happiness, but that doesn't change the fact that every single human heart yearns to *be* happy.

Now let's expand our thinking about happiness and bring God into the equation. I'm constantly struck by how many people have a distorted image of God. They picture him as some sort of celestial killjoy, or an aloof and distant being, or an eternal clockmaker who wound up creation, set it in motion, and left it at that. The truth is this: God is the happiest of all beings! And his happiness is total and eternal. Nothing can diminish or even perturb his happiness.

Now, remember that we said that God *is* love. And as we saw in the previous chapter, God brought us into being out of love. But that's not all. He actually made us in his own image and likeness. Wouldn't he want a being so made—so loved—to be happy just as he is happy?

Again, you shouldn't have to think too hard. Of course he would! Here's an indisputable truth: God made you and me and everyone else to be happy. In fact, he wants you and me and everyone else to be happy far more than we want to be happy. That's how good God is—infinitely good.

But of course, there's a problem. If God wants us to be happy, why is our world filled with unhappiness? Why do even the most fortunate struggle to find happiness, only to see it slip through their fingers when they think they have located it?

Maybe one of the reasons is that we don't always know what genuine happiness consists of. We don't know where to look for it or how to find it, and sometimes (maybe often!) we don't recognize it when it's staring us in the face. We're very good at looking for happiness in all the wrong places, and that means we need a helping hand in our search. Otherwise we're likely to spend our lives drifting from one failed attempt to find happiness to another.

So where should we look for that helping hand? The only logical answer is that we look to the source of whatever happiness we have known—the source of all the happiness there has ever been and ever will be. In other words, we look to God. It's only reasonable to assume that the God who made us in his image and likeness is the only one who can reveal to us how to find the happiness for which he created us.

Clues in Scripture to finding happiness

Let's begin by following the clues that God has given us. God never leaves us in the dark. He never fails to give us a powerful series of signposts to follow, and the most important of those signposts are always found in Holy Scripture. So we're going to return to Scripture in our search for real happiness. This time we'll take a look at the second creation story in the Book of Genesis.

There's one important thing to keep in mind, and we've mentioned it before: when we read the early stories of Genesis, we must be aware that we're dealing with inspired poetry. It's incredibly rich in symbol, metaphor, mystery, and meaning. However, we must never think it is a conventional historical narrative.

With that in mind, let's dive into the story of the creation of the first man.

Clue #1: God's breath

[T]hen the LORD God formed man of dust from the ground, and breathed into his nostrils the breath of life; and man became a living being. And the LORD God planted a garden in Eden, in the east; and there he put the man whom he had

formed. And out of the ground the LORD God made to grow
every tree that is pleasant to the sight and good for food, the
tree of life also in the midst of the garden, and the tree of the
knowledge of good and evil. (Genesis 2:7-9)

We see that God fashions man out of the ground—out of
dust—and then he breathes life into that man. Something special is happening here. In fact, it's unique! It's utterly unlike
God's many other creative acts that are recounted in Genesis. Here God animates the first man by breathing his own
breath into him.

Breath and *life* were essentially synonymous words to the
biblical writers. Not only that, but *life* and therefore *breath*
were all but synonymous with the soul, the very essence
of someone. So this passage can be read as God breathing
something of himself—something divine—into the man at
the first moment of the man's existence. This is to show us
clearly that God's human creation is unique and uniquely
loved. God treats this creature—you and I—in a very special and intimate way.

God's act of breathing on man is of major significance in
the Bible. There are only two other places where he does anything like this. The first is found in the book of the prophet
Ezekiel. God leads the prophet into a valley that is strewn
with the bones of long-dead people. There is not even a hint
of life among the bones, which are bleached white and as
dry as the desert. Yet in a moment, God restores life, and the
bones become living people again—or almost living people.
As with the man in Genesis, something is still missing. God
says to Ezekiel:

"Prophesy to the breath [or spirit], prophesy, son of man, and say to the breath, Thus says the Lord GOD: Come from the four winds, O breath, and breathe upon these slain, that they may live." So I prophesied as he commanded me, and the breath came into them, and they lived, and stood upon their feet, an exceedingly great host. (37:9-10)

So again God sends breath to confer life—a unique type of life—on his human creation.

The other place in which God breathes on man is more familiar to us and also more significant. It occurs in the twentieth chapter of the Gospel of St. John. Here's the story:

It is Easter morning, but the apostles as yet know nothing of Jesus' resurrection. Locked in the Upper Room, they are a fearful, demoralized band. Then Jesus, who they know to be dead, is suddenly present. He is alive and really *present* with them!

Jesus came and stood among them and said to them, "Peace be with you." When he had said this, he showed them his hands and his side. Then the disciples were glad when they saw the Lord. Jesus said to them again, "Peace be with you. As the Father has sent me, even so I send you." And when he had said this, he breathed on them, and said to them, "Receive the Holy Spirit." (20:19-22)

On the surface of things, this seems strange, perhaps even inexplicable. Why does Jesus do this? Why does he breathe on the apostles, and why does the Gospel writer make sure to tell us that he did? Perhaps if we hadn't read the creation stories in Genesis and the passage from Ezekiel, we wouldn't know. But we should know now. We should know that the breath of God confers life.

In the original creation narrative (as well as in the Book of Ezekiel), God breathes on man not only so that man can live but so that he can live a type of life that transcends that of the animals and plants around him. Now we see Jesus, newly risen from the dead. He has begun the work of restoring God's creation, which has been corrupted by man's sin and rebellion. Thus Jesus—God incarnate—breathes on man exactly as God did in the Book of Genesis.

In a sense, this passage from the Gospel of St. John becomes another creation story. As God breathed on man to bestow on him life in the Book of Genesis, so Jesus breathes on man to bestow on him a new and abundant life, to begin man's re-creation and reconciliation with the God against whom he has rebelled.

So this act of God breathing on man is of real importance. We see in it God's desire for an extreme intimacy between himself and humankind. Think about it: he wants that relationship to be so intimate that his breath is our very life. How much more intimate is it possible to get?

Clue #2: The garden

Returning to the Book of Genesis, we see that after God has breathed life into the man, he places that man in a garden: "The LORD God took the man and put him in the garden of Eden to till it and keep it" (2:15). This is yet another indication of God's great love for us, although we rarely stop to think of it that way. God has created an entire world—an entire universe, really. Yet he prepares a special place for his human creation, one that is superior to every other place in the world. This is not just an ordinary garden; it's a paradise, a place where every need is fulfilled. It's a place without want or sorrow.

And as we saw in the last chapter, the idea of a garden also figures prominently in the gospel accounts of the passion and death of Jesus: Jesus prays in a garden before giving himself over to suffering and death, and he is laid in another garden after his crucifixion. Everything begins in a garden in the Book of Genesis, and now we see that everything's going to "re-begin" in a garden, starting at the moment of Jesus' resurrection.

Let's take a look at another scene from the Gospel of St. John. It's that moment early on the first Easter Sunday morning when a grieving Mary Magdalene comes to the garden to anoint the body of Jesus:

> Saying this, she turned round and saw Jesus standing, but she did not know that it was Jesus. Jesus said to her, "Woman, why are you weeping? Whom do you seek?" Supposing him to be the gardener, she said to him, "Sir, if you have carried him away, tell me where you have laid him, and I will take him away." (20:14-15)

What's John's point here? Well, he has many, but one of them is that Mary is not completely wrong when she thinks of Jesus as a gardener. Jesus truly is not just a gardener but *the Gardener*. As God once walked in the cool of the day with Adam and Eve in the garden he had created for them, so now God incarnate, as he refashions his creation, walks with Mary Magdalene, one of his most faithful disciples, in the cool of the morning on the day of his resurrection. We see here a sign of a return to that earlier state of humankind's existence, when we were not estranged from God.

Back to the second creation story in the Book of Genesis: we see that God gives the man the trees and plants and tells him to till the soil. What do we notice here? Read carefully, because it's easy to miss. We see that God does not expect man to lounge around all day; he's supposed to till the soil. So work is not in any way a product of the fall. Toil and exhaustion are, but work itself is not. Man was created to work.

Why? Because we are created in the image and likeness of God, and work offers us a way of participating in God's creativity. God creates matter. We use that matter to make tools and objects and works of art. God offers us through our work a way of being a little bit like him.

Clue #3: A helper

Let's turn our attention to verses 18 through 25:

> Then the LORD God said, "It is not good that the man should be alone; I will make him a helper fit for him." So out of the ground the LORD God formed every beast of the field and every bird of the air, and brought them to the man to see what he would call them; and whatever the man called every living creature, that was its name. The man gave names to all cattle, and to the birds of the air, and to every beast of the field; but for the man there was not found a helper fit

for him. So the LORD God caused a deep sleep to fall upon the man, and while he slept took one of his ribs and closed up its place with flesh; and the rib which the LORD God had taken from the man he made into a woman and brought her to the man. Then the man said,

> "This at last is bone of my bones
>   and flesh of my flesh;
> she shall be called Woman,
>   because she was taken out of Man."

Therefore a man leaves his father and his mother and cleaves to his wife, and they become one flesh. And the man and his wife were both naked, and were not ashamed. (Genesis 2:18-25)

Pay careful attention to the first words of this passage: "Then the LORD God said, 'It is not good that the man should be alone.'" You might notice something startling here. In the previous chapter, God has been creating one thing after another until, at the end of the sixth day, he has created the entire universe and everything in it. Each time he creates, he declares his creation "good," and on the final day he declares it "very good." Yet here we are in the second creation story, and something about that has changed. Something that is not good (or not as good as it could be) has entered creation: "It is not good that the man should be alone." God sees that the situation he has placed his favorite creation in is not yet complete, for the man is alone. In all of creation, which is now teeming with life, he does not have a helper who is "fit for him."

(And on that note, let's take a brief time out and discuss the word *helper*. It's a problem to many people, especially those who consider the biblical texts to have enshrined within them a powerful misogyny—an understanding of woman as being inferior to and subservient to man. Yes, it sure seems that the text could be read in exactly that way—at least the English version of it could be. But God does not create a servant to bring the man his slippers and the remote control. The Hebrew word we translate as "helper" is *ezer*. This is a word used only twenty-one times throughout the Bible. Sixteen of those times, *ezer* is actually applied to God, when he helps human beings. When we see *ezer* used in the Bible, we should know it never refers to someone in an inferior position but to someone who offers essential—often life-saving or life-transforming—aid. So anyone who understands how that Hebrew word was used knows that this verse is not the place to look for sexism in the Bible. I hope that clears up that particular problem. Now back to the main story.)

So what does God do once he has declared that it is not good that man should be alone? He brings man a long line of animals as potential helpers. All of them (even the mightiest and the cutest—the hippo, the poodle, or my personal favorite, the panda) strike out quickly. So do we conclude from this that God isn't quite sure what the man needs?

We could, I suppose, but there's a big problem with that: God is all-knowing, so he has to know what the man needs. Yet he acts as if he doesn't. What's going on here?

God knows exactly not just *what* but *who* the man needs. He's known that since before time began, and he could have created woman at any point. But he didn't. Instead he draws things out, letting the man search for a suitable helper and come to the conclusion that no such helper exists. The man now knows that the world still lacks what he needs the most. And when he realizes this, the man becomes more aware not just of his aloneness but of his uniqueness in creation—of his need for something like himself that he cannot find in the whole universe of animals, plants, and matter.

Do we see our own lives reflected here? How often have we felt a great need for something—a need that not only remained unfulfilled but just grew and grew? God often makes us aware of certain types of needs and then does exactly the opposite of what we want. We want our needs immediately satisfied; instead God intensifies our desires.

This may seem like divinely inflicted torture, but there's a purpose to it. As someone once put it, "To be a creature is to be one giant desire." And that's about as perfectly stated as it could be.

God acts in ways that show us that there are specific non-negotiable needs that are part and parcel of our lives. And then he shows us that the world cannot satisfy those deep and aching needs. He lets us know the truth of our lives: that our deepest desires can be satisfied only by him, because that's the way we were made.

Now, returning to the man who needs a helper, let's ask ourselves exactly what he needs help for. He's living in paradise, and he has an intimate relationship with God. That sounds pretty good to me. What help can he possibly need? Another and probably better way of asking the question is this: Why is it not good that the man should be alone?

The answer to that is as simple as it is profound: the man needs help to be human. On his own, he cannot be fully human, because man is made for relationship, for friendship, and ultimately for love. And none of those things is possible if he is alone. To be what he was made to be, he needs another person, someone who is like him but is different.

Let's clarify exactly what the man was created for. He was made first to be loved and then to love (in that order!). And here we have arrived at one of the deepest truths about what it means to be made in the image and likeness of God.

We need love to be happy

In the last chapter, we had a list of eight items that together encompassed much of what it means to be made in the image and likeness of God. This element, to be loved and to love, is so important that I wanted to consider it separately. It could, however, be the first element on any such list, because none of us can be fully human without it.

But why is that the case? Why can man not be fully human alone or without love?

To answer this incredibly important question, we must look to the God in whose image we are made. Who is this God? Is he some celestial king who reigns in solitary splendor, infinitely removed from his creation? No, absolutely not! The most fundamental thing we can say about God is that God is three—three persons, Father, Son, and Holy Spirit, who live in an eternal relationship that someone once described as a "reckless exchange of love."

Now, we're liable to interpret *reckless* to mean something like "careless," but that is by no means the case. What we're really talking about here is a love that holds absolutely nothing back. That love is the divine reality. The Father gives everything to the Son, and the Son gives everything to the Father. Their love is so intense and so complete that the mutual love between the two "spirates" (meaning "breathes") the Third Person of the Trinity.

We cannot fully reflect the divine image (or understand ourselves) without understanding something of the reality of God's nature. If we don't know that God's nature is to love in a way that is absolute and total, or that his very essence is love, we will get almost everything wrong. Once again, God has nothing to do with that solitary, distant king. God's existence is always communal, always an eternal relationship.

And that's why it's not good for the creature made in God's image to be alone. Only in relationship—only in being loved by and loving others—does it become possible for man to reflect the God who made him and become what God created him to be. Only by being loved and by loving can the human person find happiness.

And that's the reason God must provide someone for the man to be in relationship with—someone who can love him and whom he can love. God does this by creating woman. It's important to see that he creates her from the same "stuff" as he did the man, thus showing their absolute equality.

In fact, God actually creates woman from the man. He causes a deep sleep to come over the man and then creates woman from the man's rib—from the very matter of the man's body and from the part of his body that actually guards his heart. And then he brings the woman to the man and presents her to him. In this act of presenting the newly created woman to the man, we can see the model for all the countless weddings that have taken place over all of history. It's as if God is saying to the man, "This is my beloved daughter, the apple of my eye. Love her, care for her, and she will love and care for you."

At this moment—the moment the man ceases to be alone—he is transformed, and Scripture shows him doing something that indicates his humanity is now complete. No, much more than that, Scripture shows him euphoric! The man, for the first time in the Bible, when he sees the woman, speaks! It is as if he is overcome with emotion, and he exclaims,

> "This at last is bone of my bones
> and flesh of my flesh." (Genesis 2:23a)

In other words, he instantly recognizes in the woman someone who is like him. He grasps that he is related to the woman in a way that he is not related to the rest of creation. It's as if he is saying, "This one is at last like me!"

Then he immediately names the woman:

> "[S]he shall be called Woman,
> because she was taken out of Man." (Genesis 2:23)

Now, we might be tempted to think that in naming the woman, he is displaying some sort of dominion over her, since he has previously named the animals. But something is very different here. In naming the woman, he actually names himself. In other words, the man only understands who he is in light of her.

Remember that the man has had no real name until this moment. So far he has been called only the "adam," which is a word that is related to the word for ground or earth, referring to the way in which he was created—out of the "dust of the earth." It's like calling him a clump of earth. The man has no real identity—no real humanity—until the woman is present.

In the original Hebrew, the word for woman is *isha,* and the word for man is *ish.* They share the same root word; one is the feminine form of the word, and the other is the masculine. Just by standing there in front of the man, the woman proclaims to him this glorious truth: "You're made for me, and I'm made for you. That's why I'm here, so that we can love each other. That's why God created me. That's why God created you." Pope St. John Paul II used to refer to this as one aspect of "the 'prophetic' character of women" (*Mulieris Dignitatem,* 29).

Let's be clear: this doesn't mean that only married people can be happy. The Bible gives us the male-female relationship as the primary human loving relationship, but it is far from the only one. There are many ways to love and be loved. The Bible is simply telling us that a human life without love is not just severely incomplete but meaningless.

So now we've discovered what we need to be happy: we need love. But what is love?

You might think you understand the answer to that question, but don't be too sure. Our culture has done a spectacular job of confusing us when it comes to words and concepts.

We've already said that many words relating to our faith and to the way we live in general have been mutated in one way or another. They've been given meanings different from the ones they should have and always have had.

Well, the word we're considering now, *love,* perhaps more than any other word, is a victim of this mutating process. If we are to truly understand what love is, we must try to forget about the version we know from movies, TV, and popular songs. Then we must accept that in its essence, *love* is a word that properly belongs to God. Why?

I'm sure you can answer that question easily, because we've already spoken about it several times. But in case you've forgotten, here it is: love is a word that belongs to God, because God *is* love. Therefore, the only way we can truly understand love is by understanding who God is. God is our only real measure of love. He is the only standard we can use.

Here's the definition of love that the Church most often uses: to love is to will the objective good of another. Does that seem strange to you? Does the fact that it has nothing to do with feelings or emotions seem weird?

It might, but feelings and emotions are subjective and short-lived. True love is neither; true love is rooted in the will, not the emotions, in the determination to do whatever is best for the one who is loved, no matter what the cost might be. I know for myself that I most learn what love is when there are no feelings or when the feelings for the other person aren't all that warm and fuzzy.

The next verse in the Book of Genesis focuses on God's plan for marriage: "Therefore a man leaves his father and his mother and cleaves to his wife, and they become one flesh" (2:24). That verse isn't talking about where a newly married couple is going to live. It's saying that when two people really love each other, they find a new center to their lives in that love, a new focal point. Their families of origin are no longer their center; the new family they are establishing becomes that and remains that for the rest of their lives.

And then the text continues, saying that the two "become one flesh." This doesn't refer simply to the obvious, to sexual intercourse. It refers more properly to the totality of marriage. Marriage—real marriage—is a total partnership in life—in affection, in mind, and in body. In marriage, everything one has belongs to the other as well.

Now look at the last verse of the second chapter of the Book of Genesis, which shows us what the fruit of that total partnership is supposed to be: "And the man and his wife were both naked, and were not ashamed" (2:25).

What does that mean? Honestly, I don't know. I have never known this. Thanks to the fall, or "the big thud," none of us has known it, save Mary. The history of the relationship between men and women since the fall has been one marked by using and being used, by exploiting and being exploited, by objectifying and being objectified, by lusting after and desiring to be lusted after, by dominating and conniving in being dominated.

But the Scriptures offer us here a picture of what it once was like, way back at the beginning. There really was a time when there was only pure love between man and woman; there was no fear at all, no mistrust, no suspicion of any ulterior motives. And the good news of the gospel is that, even now, God's plan for marriage can happen, even though we have been marred by original sin. Though we may not be what we once were in the Garden of Eden, by God's grace we can overcome the temptations we all have to use others and can love instead.

We need to trust God to be happy

But why is that pure love gone? That's the topic of the next chapter, but we're on a roll, so we're going to have a little preview. Let's take a look at verses 16 and 17 in the second chapter of Genesis: "And the LORD God commanded the man, saying, 'You may freely eat of every tree of the garden; but of the tree of the knowledge of good and evil you shall not eat, for in the day that you eat of it you shall die.'"

This is a very confusing piece of the story, and it raises many questions. We can imagine someone asking, "Are we really supposed to believe that God planted some tree in the middle of a garden somewhere and for no discernible reason said to Adam and Eve that they could do anything they wanted—that there were really no limits on them at all—except that they couldn't eat the fruit of this one tree? And then when they did eat it, God got so angry that he kicked them out of the garden and killed them? That's the silliest thing I've ever heard in my whole life, and I'm out of here."

Well, I would agree with that imaginary skeptic. But that's not at all what God is revealing here. First of all, let me remind you once again: we're in a poetic world in Genesis, one that expresses itself with symbol. In other words, the book reveals truth but not necessarily literally. So let's try to understand what "the tree of the knowledge of good and evil" really means and what it doesn't mean.

First of all, the tree is not an apple tree. It's also not a test that the first man and woman fail. It's not some arbitrary rule that God came up with on a day when he was bored and had nothing else to do. It doesn't even mean that before eating the fruit of the tree, the man and woman didn't understand the difference between good and evil.

Here's what the tree really does mean—and it should come as no surprise to anyone who's read the earlier chapters in this book. In the tree of the knowledge of good and evil, God is offering a relationship to the man and the woman. He is offering his friendship. But friendship requires trust. It's as if God is saying to the man and the woman, "I've given you everything here. I've given you each other. I've given you your very selves. Here's what I need from you. I need you to trust me completely."

So far, so good. Now let's focus on what eating the fruit of this tree actually means. What does eating anything mean? To eat something is to experience it deeply, to taste it, to assimilate it, to break it down within you and make it part of you. In the case of the tree of the knowledge of good and evil, it's to break down and make part of you the knowledge of good and evil, or perhaps we could say more simply that it's to assimilate the origins of all reality.

How's that for a gargantuan task? I think we all know that man can't do that. And the reason man can't do that has nothing whatsoever to do with God's not permitting him to do it. Man is a creature, and a creature can't know the origins of all reality. A creature can't determine for itself what is ultimately good and evil. Only God has the capacity for that. Only God knows the origins of all reality and what is ultimately good and evil. So to eat of this tree is to claim something that no creature has the right or the ability to claim: it is to claim to be God.

And if I make myself to be God, what does that mean? It means that I've rejected the real God, set myself up as his replacement, and cut myself off from the very source of my being. What does *that* mean? It means this: if God is life and I cut myself off from life, I die. That's the truth that is really being shown to us here.

So the warning not to eat of the fruit of the tree "lest you die" is not what it seems to be. It's not a warning from some authority figure saying, "Here are the rules, and you'd better follow them, because if you don't follow them, I'm going to be so ticked off that I'm going to kill you." That's the way these words have been read by countless people, but it's very, very wrong.

God is not a distant authority figure. He's more like a mother, who out of love for her child says, "I know the red stove looks really attractive, but don't put your hand on it, because if you touch the stove, you'll burn yourself, and that will be very painful." Of course, the mother's not saying that *she* will burn the child because she's angry he disobeyed her. She's saying that the stove is dangerous and that the child must understand that and be careful around it. The mother warns the child out of concern and love.

That's what God is doing here. He's saying, "I made you; I'm your Father; you're my child. Trust me. Don't do that. If you do that, you'll die, and I don't want you to die. I did not make you for death."

So the tree is a gift. It is the necessary gift that enables the relationship, the friendship, between the man and the woman and God to continue. But the man and woman eventually reject the gift. We call this "the fall," but it's honestly nothing of the sort. It's really a rebellion. They choose disobedience, and in the process, they quite literally unleash hell into human reality and bring about the single worst day in the history of the universe.

And that is the human story. It is played out in the early pages of the Bible, and it repeats itself over and over again throughout those sacred texts, in countless variations. It is also played out in your life and in mine—in fact, in the life of every human being—every day. The good God, the loving Father who made the man and the woman and called them to friendship, stands before each of us at every moment of our lives, asking the same question: Will you trust me?

To say yes and to trust in God is to open oneself to ultimate happiness, to a kind of loving relationship with God that fulfills all our desires and enables us to love and be loved by others. To say no is to cut oneself off from the only source of happiness there is and to live a life marked by emptiness and meaninglessness.

How do you respond?

Questions for Reflection and Discussion

1. If someone asked you where to find happiness, what would you say? Have you ever searched for happiness in the wrong place? What did you learn?

2. Because we are made in the image and likeness of God, our work reflects the creativity of God. How does this change the way you view your work?

3. God sometimes makes us aware of a need and then lets that need intensify for a while before answering it. If this has happened for you, how did you react? What did you learn about God?

4. Man was made first to be loved and then to love. How does reflecting on the nature of God deepen your understanding of this truth? How does your own experience with loving and being loved help you to understand it?

5. Why do we need to trust God in order to be happy? Where in your life do you struggle with trusting God?

4. Bridge Out

The Bridge to God Is Destroyed through Our Rebellion

With this chapter, we've reached a critical stage in the story—the part when humanity rebels against its Creator, changing the relationship between God and man catastrophically. As you can see, the title of this chapter is "Bridge Out," and I think that's a perfect metaphor for what happened: through his own rebellion, man destroyed the bridge to God, leaving himself stranded and in a seemingly hopeless situation.

But before we discuss that bridge and its tragic collapse, let's take a look at where we've been so far. We've seen that God created everything. We've also seen that he created you and me—all human beings—in his image and likeness. And we know that being so created means that we are made for a special relationship with our Creator—so special that God wants us to be divinized. Astonishingly, God actually wants us to partake of his own life.

So far it all sounds great. But if what I've just said is true—and it is—why doesn't it reflect life as we know it? If the good God created everything, and if everything he made is (or at least was) good, why is there so much evil, suffering, and death in our lives? Why does our world seem so broken?

Well, that's where the bridge and its demolition come in. That's the big question that we're going to address in this chapter. And just as we've done in the previous couple of chapters, we're going to the Book of Genesis looking for answers.

We're heading to chapter three of Genesis this time. It contains the famous story of the fall, which we've also called "the big thud." Those terms, however, could imply that there was something accidental about it. There wasn't. It was a rebellion, a rejection. It was also a well-planned and perfectly executed attack by an implacable enemy. It's essential that we be aware of this enemy and his attack as we move forward.

Our goals in this chapter are only two, but they're very important, so keep them in mind:

- to expose the maliciousness of that enemy and his horrific attack
- to reveal God's extraordinary response to our rebellion and rejection of him

Let's begin with the enemy. We have to be careful not to think of him in abstract terms. Abstractions won't work here. We're talking about the enemy of the entire human race, but we're also talking about more than that. We're talking about *your* enemy and *my* enemy.

This enemy's attack is always very personal, aimed at an individual's unique weaknesses. That makes him formidable. He also likes to work in shadows—"undercover," so to speak—so that we are unaware that he's there. This makes him an even more difficult opponent. Yet we are far from alone in our fight, because our Father wants to shine a spotlight on this shadowy enemy for us.

Let's examine what God shows us about the enemy. We must be very careful to see exactly what is exposed—to see that enemy for exactly who and what he is. In order to do that, we need to consider five points:

- Who is this enemy?
- Why did he rebel?
- What is his lie? (And I'm convinced there is only one lie.)
- What is his endgame?
- Why is sin so serious?

Who is this enemy?

To find out who our enemy is, let's look at what Genesis says:

> Now the serpent was more subtle than any other wild creature that the LORD God had made. He said to the woman "Did God say, 'You shall not eat of any tree in the garden'?" (3:1)

In these two sentences, we meet the enemy, and we see right away that he is different from the other wild creatures in that he is "more subtle." Some translations call him "the shrewdest of all the wild beasts." Others call him the "most crafty" of the creatures God has made. No matter what translation is used, it is clear that the serpent is far from innocent. The question he asks of the woman shows us that he plans and even plots. We also see that he uses words to manipulate the creatures with whom he interacts.

But where does this serpent come from? Let's examine a few verses taken from the first chapter of the Book of Genesis to find out:

> And God said, "Let the earth bring forth living creatures according to their kinds: cattle and creeping things and beasts of the earth according to their kinds." And it was so. And

God made the beasts of the earth according to their kinds and the cattle according to their kinds, and everything that creeps upon the ground according to its kind. And God saw that it was good. (1:24-25)

Included among the things that God creates on the sixth day is "everything that creeps upon the ground." Stop there, and give that some thought. What creeps on the ground? Snakes do—among many other things. That's important. Why? Because this biblical verse shows us that the serpent who questions the woman is a creature—not a competitor—of God. It reminds us that there is nothing that does not owe its existence to God and that is outside of his control. It tells us something else as well: the serpent, like everything else God created, was good—at least he was so originally.

Sometimes we're tempted to see reality almost like a movie, where's there's a good god and a rival evil god fighting it out. But the truth is that there is only one God, and he is good. Our enemy is not equal to God; he's a creature, and he was once good, like everything else the good God created.

But what happened to this once good creature? To answer that, we have to turn from the early chapters of the Book of Genesis and go all the way to the end of the story: the Book of Revelation, which is the last book of the Bible. All of Revelation is worth careful reading and meditation, and I recommend it highly, but right now we're going to concentrate on only one verse:

And the great dragon was thrown down, that ancient serpent, who is called the Devil and Satan, the deceiver of the whole world—he was thrown down to the earth, and his angels were thrown down with him. (12:9)

So we find that, at the very end of the story, God reveals the identity of someone who first shows up at the beginning of the story (in Genesis 3). We learn that the enemy, now described as both a serpent and a dragon, once dwelled in heaven. That's another way of saying that he was an angel—a good angel. In other words, the creature we first encounter as a serpent—a thing that creeps upon the earth—was once a member of the heavenly courts with Michael, Gabriel, and Raphael. But clearly he is very far from heaven now. He no longer has a right to be there; he has been cast down. He opposes the God who created him. Why?

Before we look at the reason why he rebelled, let's ask who he is. The names Scripture gives for him help us here. His names reveal his character, his nature.

The first name the Bible gives us is the devil, which is a word derived from the Greek word *diabolos*. That word means "divider." The enemy splits things, or at least he tries to do so. What things? Marriages, families, parishes, friendships, and nations. In other words, the devil splits relationships.

The first human relationship the devil wants to split is the most fundamental one: marriage. Marriage is the relationship from which all other relationships flow. It is the first cell of society, and so it is the devil's first target. But it is hardly his last. Anything the devil can get his hands on, he wants to split. As we think about the many divisions in our world—of the unending conflicts between groups and nations—we can see not only that the enemy is still active but that he does his work well.

The enemy is indeed a divider, but he is more than that, and he has many other names. The Bible also tells us that he is called Satan, as we just saw in the Book of Revelation. This name comes from a Hebrew word that means the "adversary" or the "accuser."

The enemy not only divides, but he also accuses. Whom does he accuse? First of all, he accuses God. But before we discuss that, let's take a look at the other objects of the devil's accusations: he accuses me and you, every one of us. How many times have you heard, in one way or another, this voice saying something like, "Do you really think God will forgive you after what you've done?" or "All that talk about the love of God . . . that's not for you. That's for other people—better people." Sound familiar?

Who hasn't experienced that kind of accusation? It seems to come from nowhere, and it is very effective at making us doubt ourselves. But the accusation doesn't come out of nowhere. It comes from an adversary, an enemy whose very nature is to accuse, an enemy who hates you and me.

Why did he rebel?

Now that we know who this enemy is, let's move on to our second point and try to discover his motives. Why did he rebel? In fact, why does he remain in constant, eternal rebellion? Why would a good angel who dwelled in heaven—in the very presence of God—choose to rebel and leave?

The answer is startling, alarming, and not entirely clear from the story so far. In a good movie or book, the antagonist sometimes shows up at the beginning but without explanation. We don't really know why he's there, and we don't yet have the information we need in order to understand why he's so bent on destruction. It's only later, as the story unfolds, that we find out what went wrong.

So it is in Scripture. The serpent shows up in Genesis, chapter 3, as a tempter, and in the Book of Revelation we see him as a fierce and destructive dragon. But what happened to make him so? The Book of Wisdom—about halfway through the Bible— gives us some help. In this Old Testament book, we read the following disturbing words:

> [B]ut through the devil's envy death entered the world, and those who belong to his party experience it. (2:24)

Here we have it: the motive for his rebellion is envy. If we have forgotten what envy is, the *Catechism* is quick to remind us: "Envy is a capital sin. It refers to the sadness at the sight of another's goods and the immoderate desire to acquire them for oneself, even unjustly" (2539).

So the angel who became the divider, the accuser, and the adversary was envious, and his envy became the source of his rebellion. But of whom was he envious, and why?

People almost always assume that he was envious of God, but they're wrong. This angel wasn't envious of God. He was envious of us—of you and of me! He was envious of the human race.

Tradition holds that God made the angelic host aware of his plan for his creation, a plan that culminates in his favorite creature, us, being divinized, sharing forever in his own eternal life. That special friendship and that special destiny are the sources of the angel's envy. He becomes outraged that creatures as weak as we are, in comparison to the majesty and intellect of the angels, should be favored over him. His anger and envy are so great that he rebels.

And he does not rebel alone. As we already read in the Book of Revelation, "He was thrown down to the earth, and his angels were thrown down with him" (12:9). Tradition tells us that a third of the angelic host rebel with the angel who became Satan. In their outrage, they go to war against the creatures they envy—against us.

What is his lie?

Now let's look at the third of our five points about the enemy: What is the great lie that he uses when he goes to war against us? Again, the answer is found in the third chapter of the Book of Genesis. But before we look at the Scriptures, let's approach the situation with an analogy that I find particularly helpful.

In sports, at least at the higher levels, an important part of preparing for a game is looking at "game film." This game film shows the strategies, strengths, and weaknesses of the opponent. If you can get them down, you enter into the game better prepared to win.

Well, God wants us to win, and so he gives us a game film (of sorts) in Genesis, chapter 3. Genesis 3 doesn't simply reveal what happened a long time ago to our first parents; it reveals what *always* happens. This is the strategy of the enemy, our enemy. Let's "watch" attentively then, to see what God is showing us.

> [The serpent] said to the woman, "Did God say, 'You shall not eat of any tree of the garden'?" And the woman said to the serpent, "We may eat of the fruit of the trees of the garden; but God said, 'You shall not eat of the fruit of the tree which is in the midst of the garden, neither shall you touch it, lest you die.'" But the serpent said to the woman, "You will not die. For God knows that when you eat of it your eyes will be opened, and you will be like God, knowing good and evil." (3:1b-5)

It all starts so harmlessly, or so it seems. A simple, almost innocuous question becomes the first step toward disaster. That famous question is not as clear as it seems, because it's not really a question at all. The serpent says in effect, "So, God says you can't eat of any of the trees of the garden . . ." It's as if the serpent is on a fishing expedition, and he's dropping these words like bait for the woman to take. Tragically, she bites.

God is revealing something very important to us here, something we need to know to survive our own confrontations with the adversary: don't get into a dialogue with the enemy. "Have nothing to do with the 'dragon,'" is how St. John Paul II once put it (Homily at Fatima, May 13, 2000). Why?

The answer to that one is simple: because if you do, you'll lose, just as the woman in the Book of Genesis does. Once the dialogue has begun, the serpent proves that the name

Satan (the accuser) fits him perfectly. He accuses God of holding out on the woman. The serpent is saying, "If God really loved you, he'd let you eat of that tree. But he won't let you eat of that tree, because he doesn't really love you. He's holding you down, limiting you, restricting you. He knows that if you eat of that tree, you will become like him, and he doesn't want that."

This is the enemy's big lie: God doesn't love us; he's not a good Father; he's your adversary, the enemy of your freedom and your happiness. What makes the devil's lie so evil is that it's a direct denial of the reality for which God made us. God *does* want us to share in his life, to be divinized.

Like so many of us, the woman falls for the lie. She eats the fruit and then hands it to the man, who is suddenly—inexplicably—present. He appears to have been there the whole time! This is the greatest sin of omission in history. The man should have been caring for and loving the woman, saying to her, "Don't listen to him! We know God is good and that he loves us."

What happens when they eat the fruit? The serpent's prediction actually comes true, and their eyes are opened. But the prediction comes true in a way they never anticipated: they don't become like God; instead they become aware of their own nakedness. They look at each other in a new way. Whereas once they "were naked, and were not ashamed" (Genesis 2:25), suddenly they catch each other looking with a look they have never seen before, a look that makes them afraid. "Naked, and . . . not ashamed" is a reminder of what God intends the relationship between a man and a woman to be: one that does not involve the use of one by the other, one that does not involve objectification, fear, or a sense of threat. The divider has changed all that. In fact, he's destroyed it.

We called this text, Genesis 3, "game film." God gives it to us to show us how the enemy works and what the results of his actions invariably are. In other words, God gives us this story so we can prepare. Our Father wants us to know and understand the strategy of our constant enemy. As we said earlier, this story not only shows us what happened; it shows us what always happens. This is what the enemy does: he accuses God; he places him in suspicion, tempting us to distrust him, so as to keep us from the happiness he *knows* God has for us. And all because he is envious of us.

What is his endgame?

Now let's move on to the fourth point: the endgame of the enemy. Before we begin, however, I want to make very clear that this is serious business.

I said already that God wants to drag the enemy into the light, to expose him for what he is, to make clear his malice and hatred. Why? Because the enemy is incredibly dangerous. He is not benign in any way, and he is certainly nothing to be trifled with. That's why we must never open ourselves unnecessarily to his attacks by, for example, experimenting with the occult. The dangers are simply too great. Why would you want to invite into your home someone whose only desire is to harm you?

To my mind, the most brilliant light that the Bible shines on the enemy is found in the tenth chapter of the Gospel of St. John. This is the famous discourse in which Jesus calls himself a good shepherd who lays down his life for his sheep. He contrasts that with someone else, someone he calls simply "the thief." Let's look at the relevant verse: "The thief comes only to steal and kill and destroy. I come that they may have life, and have it abundantly" (John 10:10).

Here, exposed in a few simple words, is the devastating endgame of the enemy. His plan for you, his desire for each and every one of us, is to steal us away from the good Father. He wants to kill you; he wants to kill me. He wants to destroy us. And there's no clearer way of saying that than the way I just did.

Why is sin so serious?

On that disturbing note, let's move on to examine our fifth point. We're going to turn our gaze from the enemy himself to the seriousness of the sin he wants us to commit.

Ask yourself what sin really is. I suspect that most people think of sin the way I did when I was younger, as the breaking of a law. That's a way of looking at things that almost anyone can understand, and it's not without merit. But it's hardly a complete understanding of the matter. Let's contrast it with a different understanding of sin.

When we spoke about the fall—the first sin of humankind—we called it a rebellion. And that's really the heart of the matter. In its essence, sin is always a personal rebellion. Every sin, from humankind's first sin to the ones that are being committed all around the world at this very moment, is a personal rebellion. The *Catechism* calls sin "disobedience" (1871). It is "a revolt against God," the good Father

(*CCC* 1850). St. Augustine called it "love of oneself even to contempt of God" (1850, quoting *City of God*, 14, 28).

Consider that, and while we're at it, let's think about the biblical parable that most clearly and movingly illustrates that revolt. It's the parable of the prodigal son, and it begins this way: "There was a man who had two sons; and the younger of them said to his father, 'Father, give me the share of property that falls to me'" (Luke 15:11-12). In other words, the son is asking for his inheritance.

But wait a minute. When do people receive inheritances? Only after the death of the person who originally owned the property, and the father in this parable is clearly alive. So what is the son really saying to his father? He's saying: "Father, I wish you were dead." Whenever we sin, we are doing the same thing. We're saying to the good Father, who is the source of everything we have and are: "Father, I wish you were dead."

In other words, sin is not merely the breaking of a law. It's far, far more than that. Sin is nothing less than rejecting the one who created us for intimate friendship, whose desire is that we should share in every single thing he has.

This sin, this rejection and rebellion, unleashes hell in our world. Just watch how quickly everything falls apart because of that one act in Genesis 3. As we've already said, the relationship between man and woman is disrupted. Once they were naked and unashamed; as soon as they sin, they become fearful and afraid of each other.

Immediately there follows the breaking of the relationship between the man and the woman and God. They used to walk together in the cool of the day in friendship. Now the man and the woman hide from the God who made them.

There is even a break within the man and within the woman, a break that we've all experienced and that St. Paul speaks of eloquently: "I do not do the good I want, but the evil I do not want is what I do" (Romans 7:19).

So there you have it: constant ruptures, constant breakings apart, are the results of sin. And as if all that wasn't enough, here's the worst part: sin leads to death. St. Paul articulates this in the starkest of terms: "The wages of sin is death" (Romans 6:23). There's no ambiguity there.

This is the mess we're in, and this mess is the fruit of the rebellion of our first parents, of their listening to the lie of the enemy, of their falling prey to his accusations of God. We asked earlier, *If God is good, and everything he created he created out of love, then why are things so bad? Why is there suffering, cancer, war, abuse, and countless other evils? Why?*

Because of sin, that's why. None of these things were part of the plan; they shouldn't be here! They're here because of us, unfortunately, because of the rebellion of our first parents.

God's response to our rebellion

That's the bad news, but the gospel means "good news," and blessed be God, there is good news! Remember our second goal for this chapter? Let's look at it now: to reveal God's extraordinary response to our rebellion.

What is that response? It is his enduring love for us. We might say that God wants to give us a glimpse into his heart— an MRI of the divine heart. That glimpse is the most important thing you can take away from this chapter. The most important thing we can know about God is his great love for us.

The first signs of that response are found in Genesis 3. Let's take a look:

> And they heard the sound of the LORD God walking in the garden in the cool of the day, and the man and his wife hid themselves from the presence of the LORD God among the trees of the garden. But the LORD God called to the man and said to him, "Where are you?" And he said, "I heard the sound of you in the garden, and I was afraid, because I was naked; and I hid myself." He said, "Who told you that you were naked? Have you eaten of the tree of which I commanded you not to eat?" (3:8-11)

First of all, why does God ask where they are? Can't he see them? Of course he can; he can see everything. So that question in the text doesn't mean what it would mean if you or I were looking for someone we couldn't find. Neither does the second question necessarily mean exactly what it seems to mean. So what are those questions, really?

Before we answer that, what did you imagine God's voice sounding like as you read that passage? Was it harsh and booming? Was it demanding and angry? Was it accusatory? Did it rumble with thunder?

I suspect that one or another of those choices is how most people imagine that God would speak in such a situation. But I think God's tone is very different here. To get an idea of his real tone, let's just rewrite the first question a bit. Imagine it this way: "Where are you, . . . so that I may help you?"

Never forget that God is speaking to his favorite creature, the one he made to be divinized, the one he loves more than anything else. This favorite creature has injured himself terribly and is in great need. He's lost and can't find his way back home—back to the God and Father who loves him.

The second question is, "Have you eaten of the tree of which I commanded you not to eat?" This can almost be completed with the following sorrowful words: "Oh, no. You didn't trust me. You didn't listen to me. What have you done? You can't fathom what you have brought upon yourself. You have just welcomed suffering and death into your life, but I didn't make you for suffering and death." When we read these words, we should hear not anger in the Father's voice but deep compassion, even sadness.

Our road sign for this chapter is "Bridge Out," and once again I have to stress how apt that sign is. Once the fall—the rebellion—had taken place, the chasm between man and God was impassable from our side. We were left in a situation that was truly hopeless—at least from a human perspective. Only God could bridge that chasm, but why would he? I mean, really, why would he? After all, the creature he loved beyond all others had essentially told him, "I wish you were dead."

Yet God does bridge it. Why?

To understand how astonishing God's response is, let's try an exercise in our imagination. Imagine that you wake up and are somehow struck by the incredibly pathetic plight of worms as they slither along the sidewalk. Worms, too small and insignificant to be noticed by most people, get stepped on, their lives snuffed out in an instant. But imagine that you're moved with pity at the sight of these tiny creatures. And let's say that it is even more than pity. Let's call it a kind of love. And you decide that you want to save the worms, even though you don't have to.

And to save them, you will actually enter into their lives. You'll become one of them; you'll become a worm. You will crawl with them and eat with them. And you decide that you love these seemingly unlovable creatures so much that you're willing to lay down your life for them. You're going to let them kill you, all out of love for them. Why? So that they will become able to share in your own existence for all eternity.

Who would do that? The answer to that one is easy: nobody. *Nobody* would do it.

But God did exactly that. And let's remember that the difference between God and a human being is infinitely larger than the distance between a human being and a worm, for God is not a creature but the Creator of all things. Yet God did enter into our lives. He did lower himself an infinite distance to become one of us, in order to bridge that unbridgeable distance.

The amazing fact is that, even when we said to our Father, "I wish you were dead," he continued to love us and became one of us to save us—to save *you*, to save *me*. Out of love for us, God's Son leapt onto the stage of human history to go to war for you and me, to fight our enemy, to rebuild the bridge, to make it possible for us to get home once again. And in so doing, he proved once and for all that God is not our adversary. He is our very good Father whose love for us will never fail.

And that, my friends, is the gospel. That is the good news.

Questions for Reflection and Discussion

1. The devil accuses God of not loving us and tempts us to think that we can get something good apart from God. In what ways have you seen the enemy's strategy play out in your life? What can you do to resist these temptations?

2. What is the devil's endgame? Why is it important to know this? How does it affect your awareness of his attacks on you and your loved ones?

3. We know that the devil is a divider; the many divisions in our world offer proof of that. What divisions do you see in your own life? In the Church and in the world? How are you called to be a healer and a peacemaker in these situations?

4. We said that the fall was a rebellion. What are some of the reasons why you rebel? What do you hope to gain?

5. Why is God's response to man's rebellion so astonishing? What does this say about God's heart?

5. Bridge Restored

The Bridge is Rebuilt by God Himself through Jesus

I think we all can agree that the last chapter was a sobering read. The story of the human race's rebellion against its loving Father is poetic, but it's certainly not pretty. And when I, for one, realize that this rebellion can be summed up in one sentence: "Father, I wish you were dead," I am horrified and deeply sorrowful. That terrible sentence amounts to a complete and utter rejection of God, the one who gave us everything, including our very being. I can almost feel the bridge between God and man crashing down, leaving us not only stranded but facing endless death—eternal nothingness. It's literally the worst of all possible disasters, and it's a disaster we brought on ourselves.

That catastrophe should have ended the human story. There should be nothing left for us but to wander aimlessly in a meaningless world, cut off from God, estranged from each other, and drowning in sin. But it's not the end.

In chapter two, we talked about the differences between the God of the Bible and the pagan gods that were worshipped in the Near East. One of the main differences was that the God of the Bible is good—not selfish, not angry, not vengeful, but good and loving. It's that difference that allows the human story to go on after the fall. And it's that difference that allows the bridge to be rebuilt.

In other words, the good God does the unexpected, the unimaginable. He doesn't destroy us and start all over again. He doesn't even turn his back on us. Instead he crosses the endless chasm that separates us from him. He enters into our sinful, rebellious lives by taking on our flesh and blood. And then he rebuilds the bridge by giving his own life and becoming the bridge itself.

Think about what we're really saying here: the good God willingly accepts death to save the very ones who wished for his death, who clamored for it. Who could dare imagine such a thing?

Now we're going to take a careful look at the rebuilding of that bridge. We usually call that reconstruction job our redemption, but it's more than that—far more. Think of it as "big bang two" if you want, because it's that important. It's not just the repair of broken creation but a re-creation of wounded, sinful humanity by the God who refuses to abandon us and who loves us beyond measure.

So let's begin by establishing some goals. There are only two this time, but they're incredibly important:

- to see Mary as the new Eve
- to see more clearly Jesus' identity and what he's come to do

Why are these goals so essential? To find out, let's return to where we left off, at the fall.

Do you remember the cast of characters? There was a man and a woman and an angel (a fallen angel, whom we saw as a serpent). Well, as humanity's redemption begins, we shouldn't be too surprised to see that everything depends once again on a man and a woman and an angel.

How Mary enabled the bridge to be rebuilt

When we looked at the rebellion, the logical place to begin was with the man—God's first human creation. This time we're going to start with the woman—with Mary. Why? Because once again, it's the logical place to begin. We know that a woman (we call her Eve) became responsible for our death at the beginning of the story. Now this new woman—Mary—steps onto the stage the moment when re-creation begins.

What's her role? It's a big one, and it's the perfect inversion of Eve's, which means it's nothing less than to become responsible for our life. And that's a pretty tall order! Our redemption depends entirely on Mary of Nazareth; it wouldn't have gotten started without her. One of the Church Fathers put it this way: "Without God's Son, nothing could exist; without Mary's Son, nothing could be redeemed" (St. Anselm, Discourse 52). We can easily say that no human person has done anything that can be compared even remotely to what this woman has done. She is, in fact, the greatest human person who has ever lived or will ever live.

Let's consider the very first miracle of Jesus, a miracle that takes place in the middle of a wedding celebration in Cana (John 2:1-11). Jesus and his mother are at the wedding celebration. These celebrations didn't go on for hours, the way ours do; they went on for days! And on one of those days, embarrassingly, the wine for the guests runs out. Mary finds out about this and comes to Jesus to tell him about the problem. What does he do? He transforms 180 gallons of water into wine—or at least he does that eventually.

At first, however, Jesus does something that seems very unexpected and even out of character. Here's how St. John puts it: "When the wine failed, the mother of Jesus said to him, 'They have no wine.' And Jesus said to her, 'O woman, what have you to do with me? My hour has not yet come'" (2:2-5).

Excuse me? "Woman?" Can you imagine calling your mom that? Or if you're a mother, can you imagine your son calling you that? But Jesus isn't being rude. He's the Second Person of the Trinity. He's God. He's never rude. So why does he call his mother "woman"?

The answer isn't found in this story. Instead we have to return to the third chapter of the Book of Genesis. Let's revisit the story of the tree of the knowledge of good and evil.

Immediately after the rebellion, God speaks to the serpent and promises him this:

> I will put enmity between you and the woman,
>   and between your seed and her seed;
> he shall bruise your head,
>   and you shall bruise his heel. (Genesis 3:15)

So right here on the worst day in human history, on the very day of the rebellion, God promises to do something. What is he going to do? It might not be clear yet, but he's taking the first step in the process that will eventually undo the damage that has been done, that will rebuild the bridge.

Genesis 3:15 has actually been called "the first gospel," because in it we find God laying the groundwork for the redemption that will come about through the life, death, and resurrection of Jesus. Look at what God is saying: he's promising to undo the enemy's work—the devil's work—through a woman. The battle lines are drawn. The woman and her "seed" are on one side, and the devil and his are on the other.

It is because of this prophecy, uttered by his Father, that Jesus calls his mother "woman" at Cana. It is, we could say, the greatest title he can possibly give her. Here, at the scene of his first miracle, Jesus is identifying his mother, Mary, as "the woman," that very woman of whom God spoke in the Book of Genesis. It's as if he's saying, "*This* is the woman through whom my heavenly Father is going to put everything back together again."

Now, we said that our first goal is to see Mary as the new Eve. So let's compare these two women who seem so different. We know that the Bible frequently uses foreshadowing, and we should understand that in the story of Eve, a specific form of foreshadowing is in play. Scripture scholars have a special name for it: typology. A "type" is a person, place, event, or thing in the Old Testament that prepares us for and sheds extra light on some corresponding person, place, event, or thing in the New Testament. And the better we understand the type in the Old Testament, the better we understand the fulfillment to which it points in the New Testament.

As we look carefully at Eve, we see in her a type of Mary. How can we do that? How do we know we're not going overboard and reading things into the biblical narratives that aren't really there? Well, there are two basic reasons.

The first is that we now have two millennia of commentary on Scripture from the earliest Fathers of the Church to the present, and they all basically agree on this point. The second is that while the Bible is in one sense a collection of writings that were produced by different people in different times and places, in another and more important sense, it is a unified whole. The Bible always points in one direction. In other words, everything in it is really heading somewhere specific. It's an immense and complex story that culminates with Jesus. Every word of the Bible points in one way or another to him. And in pointing to Jesus, it also points to the woman who made Jesus' incarnation possible: Mary.

Now let's look closely at the connection between Eve and Mary. First of all, who and what was Eve?

- a virgin
- created without sin
- betrothed to a man
- visited by an angel (albeit a fallen one)
- asked a question
- disobedient to God, resulting in death for the human race

Now, who was Mary?

- a virgin
- conceived without sin
- betrothed to a man
- visited by an angel
- asked a question
- obedient to God, resulting in life for the whole human race

Because of these connections, the Church has always considered Mary to be the new Eve, the true mother of all the living. How did she become that true mother? By saying yes to the angel Gabriel. So let's take a look at the part of Scripture in which she does that, the story of the annunciation in the first chapter of the Gospel of St. Luke:

> In the sixth month the angel Gabriel was sent by God to a city of Galilee named Nazareth, to a virgin betrothed to a man whose name was Joseph, of the house of David; and the virgin's name was Mary. (1:26-27)

Do you notice how long we have to wait to learn the virgin's name? It could easily have appeared earlier, but it doesn't. This long sentence culminates with the words "and the virgin's name was Mary." It's as if all of creation is standing there, listening in, waiting for the name of the one who will make it possible for everything to be put back together. Her name is too important to simply blurt out. The evangelist is teasing it out, increasing our suspense before telling us the name of this incredible woman.

Why is this young woman from Nazareth of such importance to St. Luke? Because she did exactly what Eve did not do. She trusted God and was obedient to God.

I think we're tempted to read the story of the annunciation as if it's a done deal before it even begins. We imagine there was no chance that Mary would do anything but consent to Gabriel's strange request. But Mary, like all of us, has free will. In other words, she could have said no, and human history would have been entirely different. How do we know that Mary could have said no? Because Eve, who was created without sin, said no.

And if Mary had said no, we might be still without hope in this world. There might be no bridge home; we might still be in the hands of the enemy, who wants to steal and kill and destroy. But Mary didn't say no; she said yes! She said, "Behold, I am the handmaid of the Lord; let it be to me according to your word" (Luke 1:38). In other words, "Do to me whatever you want. I'm all yours." And it's because of those words, that willingness to trust God and give herself totally to him, that the bridge could be rebuilt. Because of those words, we owe Mary honor and thanksgiving in a way that we owe no other human person who has ever lived.

Mary's words show her willingness to put her own desires aside and completely accept the will of God. At the crucial moment, Eve chose disobedience to God and caused disaster. When Mary was faced with a similar moment, she unhesitatingly chose obedience and brought about redemption.

I once saw a bumper sticker on a car that said, "Obedient women never make history." The truth is entirely different. The truth is, without the obedience of a woman, Mary, every person's history would have no purpose, no hope. We would all be stuck in our sins.

And with that, I think we've accomplished our first goal: to see Mary as the new Eve. So let's move on to our second goal, which is to see more clearly Jesus' identity and what he's come to do.

Who is this Jesus?

First, let's return to the quotation from the Book of Genesis that deals with the woman and the serpent:

> I will put enmity between you and the woman,
>> and between your seed and her seed;
> he shall bruise your head,
>> and you shall bruise his heel. (3:15)

We now understand that Mary is the woman of whom God is speaking. The woman's "seed" should be pretty obvious; it's Jesus. Now we're ready to see who this Jesus is and figure out what he's come to do.

We're going to begin in an odd place: the evening of the first Holy Thursday, as recounted in the Gospel of St. John. Jesus has celebrated the Last Supper with his disciples and has gone to the Garden of Gethsemane to pray. Judas, who has committed himself to the greatest act of betrayal in human history, is on his way to sneak up on Jesus and arrest him. St. John writes: "So Judas, procuring a band of soldiers and some officers from the chief priests and the Pharisees, went there with lanterns and torches and weapons" (18:3).

Does anything strike you as odd about that? Imagine the scene. It is nighttime. The only light is that of the moon, which is full because it is Passover, and Passover always falls on a full moon—the paschal moon. As far as Judas and his band are aware, Jesus knows nothing of what they plan to do, so it should be easy to surprise him. But what do they do?

They carry lanterns and torches. It almost sounds as if they're coming in a procession or even a parade. They may as well have brought a brass band with them, because in the dark of night, their torches could probably be seen from miles off. Does that make sense to you? Probably not.

I suggest that this is dramatic writing by St. John. It's as if he's trying to shine a light on Jesus. John is trying to get you and me to think about where Jesus is, what he is doing, and most importantly, who Jesus is.

So let's examine those questions: Where is Jesus? What is he doing? Who is this Jesus?

Well, for one thing, he's in a garden—the Garden of Gethsemane, and we have seen that gardens are the biblical setting for both the creation and the re-creation of the world. So that's definitely important.

What's he doing? He's praying, but he's doing more than that. He's wrestling with a decision—whether he can face what must be faced to rebuild the bridge. And I would go even further on this one: he's wrestling with what he must face not just to rebuild the bridge but to literally *become* the bridge that we need to reestablish our relationship with God. The horror that awaits him is so intense, the price that he must pay is so high, that he is in agony. He is in such great torment, we are told, that he's actually sweating blood, which we know does happen to people in extreme anxiety.

In other words, he's come to the point that Eve and Adam and Mary all came to, the point at which a choice has to be made between obedience to the will of the Father and letting his own desires dictate his path. And he confronts this decision in a garden, just as Adam did. So I think we can safely conclude that St. John wants us to hear echoes of the Garden of Eden and of Adam in this scene. He wants us to see Jesus as a "new Adam"—an Adam who will do what the original one never could.

Let's look for support for this thesis in other biblical texts (remember, they all point in one direction). This time we're going to look at St. Paul's Letter to the Romans:

> Then as one man's trespass led to condemnation for all men, so one man's act of righteousness leads to acquittal and life for all men. For as by one man's disobedience many were made sinners, so by one man's obedience many will be made righteous. (5:18-19)

St. Paul is telling us two things here. The obvious one is that a new reality is being born in Jesus. Everything is starting over again with him. The other one is that Jesus functions as a second Adam. Here "one man's trespass" means the trespass of Adam, and "one man's act of righteousness" clearly refers to what Jesus did. St. Paul is telling us that, just as there is a correspondence between Eve in the Old Testament and Mary in the New, there is a similar correspondence between Adam in the Old Testament and Jesus in the New. They perform similar roles.

Yet again, the roles are inverted. Eve and Adam bring death and destruction to creation by their disobedience. Mary and Jesus bring about a new creation by their obedience.

Before we move on, let's note that in the Letter to the Romans, St. Paul calls Jesus a man. He is. But he is not a mere man. He is also God incarnate—God in the flesh. That's vital, for only God can rebuild the bridge.

From a biblical point of view, how do we know that Jesus is God? There are actually many ways. Here's one of the most important. It's the prologue of the Gospel of St. John, and its wording should sound very familiar to you:

> In the beginning was the Word, and the Word was with God, and the Word was God. He was in the beginning with God; all things were made through him, and without him was not anything made that was made. In him was life, and the life was the light of men. (1:1-4)

Here we see St. John open his Gospel with the same words with which the Book of Genesis opens: "In the beginning." That's no coincidence. John wants us to see that everything is being renewed and reborn in Christ—that it is as if God were creating the universe anew.

A few lines later, John tells us that "the Word became flesh and dwelt among us" (1:14). We have to realize that Jesus is infinitely more than mere man. He is "the Word" through whom the world came into being.

St. Paul is quick to echo St. John's assertion that Jesus actually participates in the divine being. In his Letter to the Colossians, he writes,

> [Jesus] is the image of the invisible God, the first-born of all creation; for in him all things were created, in heaven and on earth, visible and invisible, whether thrones or dominions or principalities or authorities—all things were created through

him and for him. He is before all things, and in him all things hold together. He is the head of the body, the church; he is the beginning, the first-born from the dead, that in everything he might be pre-eminent. For in him all the fullness of God was pleased to dwell, and through him to reconcile to himself all things, whether on earth or in heaven, making peace by the blood of his cross. (1:15-20)

Passages like these tell us that when we speak of Jesus, we speak of someone who is unique in the truest sense of that word. We speak not of a prophet or a wise teacher. He is not a guru of the sort that exists in Eastern religions. He is no mere good man. He is not even the greatest of men.

St. Paul tells us that "in him all the fullness of God was pleased to dwell" (Colossians 1:19). To look at Jesus, then, is to see a man but also to see infinitely more. The one who is in agony in the Garden of Gethsemane, wrestling with the decision to become the bridge and restore us to the Father, is the one through whom everything that exists has been made. The one who made the stars with a mere word is sweating blood for you and me. It staggers the mind.

What is Jesus' mission?

So why did the Second Person of the Trinity become man? He came for three very important reasons: (1) to crush the serpent's head; (2) to reveal the Father; (3) to rebuild the bridge.

Jesus crushes the serpent's head

Let's start with the first item on that list: to crush the serpent's head. Of course, that means that we are once again on our way back to the Book of Genesis. You recall that God was very explicit in saying that he would "put enmity between [the serpent] and the woman, and between [the serpent's] seed and her seed" (3:15). Well, that enmity is beginning to show itself. A major fight is brewing.

But it's not a fight between equals. "He shall bruise your head, and you shall bruise his heel" (Genesis 3:15). There's a difference between a bruise on your head and one on your heel. Which would you rather have if you had to have one? I bet it's the one on your heel. And there's a lot of hope in that.

The enemy will harass us (that's the bruise on the heel), but Scripture tells us that there will come a day when someone will crush the enemy's head, delivering him a fatal blow. Let's look at four passages in the New Testament that will help us better understand that.

The first comes from the Gospel of St. Mark; it's the first miracle in that Gospel, and it's an exorcism:

[T]here was in their synagogue a man with an unclean spirit; and he cried out, "What have you to do with us, Jesus of Nazareth? Have you come to destroy us? I know who you are, the Holy One of God." (1:23-24)

Jesus doesn't even respond to the demon, although his action clearly indicates that the answer to the second question is a resounding "Yes, I have!" He quickly casts out the demon, saving the possessed man.

There are two things to note here. The first is the ease with which Jesus casts out the demon. It is reminiscent of the ease with which God creates the universe in the Book of Genesis. God speaks, and the world is made. Jesus speaks, and the demon is banished.

The second is the love and compassion that Jesus shows to the possessed man. Jesus is God, and God's love for all those made in his own image and likeness is overwhelming.

Again, this is the first miracle recorded in Mark's Gospel, and it tells us right away that the serpent and all his forces are living on borrowed time. They can fight all they want, but they cannot win. They've been put on notice: it's only a matter of time before Jesus crushes the serpent's head.

Now let's turn to St. Matthew's Gospel. In the twelfth chapter, we read the following: "Or how can one enter a strong man's home and plunder his goods, unless he first binds the strong man? Then indeed he may plunder his house" (12:29). Who is the strong man here? The devil. And binding him is exactly what Jesus has come to do: to tie up your enemy and mine so that we can be free of the grip he has had on us since the fall.

The Letter to the Hebrews is even more explicit:

> Since therefore the children share in flesh and blood, he himself likewise partook of the same nature, that through death he might destroy him who has the power of death, that is, the devil, and deliver all those who through fear of death were subject to lifelong bondage. (2:14-15)

Remember the question in Mark's Gospel? "Have you come to destroy us?" Well, here again we have the answer: "Yes!" And in the process of destroying the one who has the power of death, Jesus does something more. What is the "life-long bondage" Hebrews speaks of? It's one of the fruits of our rebellion. It's death and the extraordinary fear we have of death. To be human is to face death and to know it, and to be human is to live in fear of death—to fear the nothing-ness that death seems to be. Jesus wants to shatter that fear, to turn death into nothing more frightening than a doorway leading us home—home to the Father.

So let's sum all this up—or rather, let's allow St. John to do that for us with our last passage, which comes from the third chapter of his first letter: "The reason the Son of God appeared was to destroy the works of the devil" (3:8).

I don't know about you, but I can't think of a way of say-ing it more clearly or succinctly than that.

Jesus reveals the Father

Jesus crushed the head of the serpent, but he came into the world to do more than that. We said that he came to reveal the Father, to show us the Father as he *really* is.

Remember that the devil's great lie is to cast God in suspi-cion; to get us to doubt God's goodness; to get us to think that God is holding out on us, that God is our adversary rather than our loving Father. Many of us go through life believ-ing that lie, or at least we believe it at one time or another. Well, in Jesus we find the definitive rebuttal to that lie and the revelation of the Father.

Let's turn again to St. John's Gospel: "Jesus said to [Thomas], 'I am the way, and the truth, and the life; no one comes to the Father, but by me'" (14:6). Many of us have heard this so many times that perhaps we no longer even think about what Jesus is saying. So let's hear it anew. Think about those words for a few minutes. When Jesus says he is the "truth," what truth is he speaking about?

He's saying that he is the most important of all truths. He is the truth about the Father. Only a few lines later, Jesus makes this very clear: "He who has seen me has seen the Father" (John 14:9). There's nothing ambiguous about that.

So take a moment and look at Jesus. If you have a crucifix within view, turn to it now and really look. Look at him as he hangs on the cross. Look at him as he breathes his last for us. Look at him as his heart explodes. Look at him as he empties himself totally in order to reconcile us to God.

And as you look, you'll see the devil's lie for exactly what it is. Is this man on the cross an adversary? Is he holding out on you? Is he holding anything back at all? Literally every drop in his body has been poured out for you and for me! It should take only a few seconds of contemplating a crucifix to see the lengths to which God is willing to go for us—the lengths to which God *has* gone for us.

A friend of mine used to say that every priest only has one real homily, and I think there's some truth to that. Well, Jesus is the "great high priest" (Hebrews 4:14), and I think that he too may have only one homily. That homily is the Father.

Jesus is always talking to us about his Father. He is always in intimate relationship with the Father, always doing what the Father does, always saying what the Father says. He's always obedient to the Father, and he lives and dies and rises again to make known once and for all, beyond all doubt, the Father's love and mercy.

Jesus rebuilds the bridge

Now let's examine the next item on our list of the reasons that Jesus came into the world, which just happens to be the topic of this entire chapter: he came to rebuild the bridge.

Remember that after the rebellion, the bridge was shattered. We could no longer reach the destiny for which we had been created, which was to be divinized—to share in God's divine life. And no human being could reconstruct that bridge. Only God could, and he did.

God didn't do it by sending a crew of angelic construction workers or by waving a magic wand. He did it by entering directly into our sinful lives and laying down his life for us. In the Gospel of St. John, Jesus says, "No one takes [my life] from me, but I lay it down of my own accord" (10:18).

Think about the wording here. Jesus says that he will "lay" his life down. It seems as if Jesus is not just rebuilding the bridge but actually *becoming* the bridge—laying himself down for us to cross over, to walk on. Later in the same Gospel, Jesus tells us this: "Greater love has no man than this, that a man lay down his life for his friends" (John 15:13).

My experience as a priest is that the deepest angst for most people is the question of identity. Who are you? Who am I? We are God's *friends. You are God's dear friend.* We must remember that when we feel abandoned, lonely, discouraged, or tempted to despair. God is the one friend who will never desert or disappoint us. He is the one who is willing to "lay down his life for his friends."

But St. John could have written that line in a slightly different way. He could have said "*sacrifice*" his life rather than "lay it down."

Sacrifice is one of the most important themes in the Bible. Throughout the Old Testament, we read of a seemingly endless number of animal sacrifices that are performed in the Jerusalem Temple. Oceans of blood were spilled there. Why? To bring about the kind of transformation that makes something that is not holy into something that is holy. The word *sacrifice* means "to make holy."

But none of those sacrifices could accomplish the transformation that humankind desperately needed. None of them could repair our broken relationship with God. The writer of the Letter to the Hebrews tells us, "[I]t is impossible that the blood of bulls and goats should take away sins" (10:4). So why did those sacrifices in the Old Testament even exist?

You should be able to answer that now. They foreshadow the ultimate sacrifice, the sacrifice that actually is effective: Jesus' sacrifice on the cross. Jesus doesn't just lay his life down for us. He literally pours out his blood for us.

There are over thirty biblical passages that refer to the pouring out of Jesus' blood. Here we'll only look at one, because it's the one we hear every time we come to Mass:

And he took a cup, and when he had given thanks he gave it to them, saying, "Drink of it, all of you; for this is my blood of the covenant, which is poured out for many for the forgiveness of sins." (Matthew 26:27-28)

This is the sacrifice of Jesus that rebuilds the bridge. It is a sacrifice in which he pours out his blood for us until there is no more blood to pour. Through the blood of Jesus, we are made new and made whole—we are made capable of holiness. And you and I can drink that blood every single day of our lives.

Jesus rebuilds the bridge by laying down his life for us, by spilling his blood for us; and he does it by actually *becoming* sin for us. There are no adequate words to convey what this really means. Even St. Paul struggles to explain it. These are his words in his Second Letter to the Corinthians: "For our sake he made him to be sin who knew no sin, so that in him we might become the righteousness of God" (5:21). The one through whom the entire universe was created *became sin out of love for you and me.*

What does that mean? It means that he absorbed into his being all of my sins, all of yours, all the sins of people who had been dead for centuries, all the sins of people who would not be born for centuries. He absorbed all the sins of everyone who has lived or will live. The holy One, the all-good One, the perfectly innocent One, *chose* to become sin for you, so you could cross the bridge and get home.

I hope we have come close to achieving our second goal, which was to understand Jesus more clearly and to have a greater grasp of what he came into our world to do. Notice I said, "Come close to achieving." Why? Because to truly achieve that goal, to really grasp the extent of Jesus' sacrifice, is more than the work of a lifetime. It's something we should never stop trying to do.

Contemplating Jesus on the cross

Have you ever seen *The Passion of the Christ*? If not, I strongly encourage you to watch it. I know many people who intentionally have not watched it because they know it will be graphic. And it is. I've seen the movie probably more than twenty times. It's one thing to read the passion narratives in the gospels; it's an entirely different thing to see with your eyes what is recorded in the text.

In the gospels, for example, we are told in one terse sentence that Jesus was scourged: "Then Pilate took Jesus and scourged him" (John 19:1). What is described in so few words, however, goes on and on in the movie. And once you see it, you'll never forget it. You hear the horrible sound of whips lacerating human flesh, the flesh of an innocent man, the flesh of the God man.

The first time I watched it, I burst into tears as I saw my God, my Lord, my Friend, being literally ripped to shreds. And all I could say, over and over again, was, "Oh, my God, . . . I am so sorry. I am so sorry. I am so sorry."

Think for a moment about the Good Friday liturgy. Every year on that day, we hear about the scourging, the crowning of thorns, and the agonizing trip up Calvary's hill. Then we walk up the aisle of the church to venerate the cross. As we do so, we hear these words being sung: "O my people, what have I done to you? How have I offended you? Answer me."

How can we answer that horrible question?

On Good Friday, and every day, we should contemplate the figure hanging on the cross—broken, bloody, and very alone. That figure is the love that rebuilt the bridge, that went so far as to become the bridge, that poured itself out until there was nothing left, that actually became our sin! That abused and dying figure is the only reason we can find our way home—can be in the presence of God and can be divinized, participating in God's own life.

If we contemplate that figure, seeking to understand what Jesus endured for us, we will face some unavoidable and deeply troubling questions: *How have I responded to this love of Jesus? How am I responding right now to this love of Jesus? How should I respond to this love of Jesus?*

Let's think about it. Let's contemplate the figure on the cross. Let's see what it took to rebuild the bridge that our selfishness, arrogance, and stupidity destroyed. Then, maybe for the first time in our lives, we will see what Mary saw as she held the infant Jesus in her arms, what she saw more than thirty years later when she again held him in her arms—this time broken, bloody, and lifeless. We will see what love is.

Rerouting

Questions for Reflection and Discussion

1. Mary said yes to God's plan because of her obedience to the Lord. Why is obedience so crucial for disciples of Christ? Where do you struggle to be obedient to what God is calling you to do?

2. How does conceiving of Jesus as a "bridge" to God change or enhance your image of him? What was required of him to become that bridge?

3. Jesus came to bind up the enemy so that we could be free of sin and death. How do you experience God's freedom in your life? What spiritual practices could lead you to even greater freedom?

4. Jesus is able to reveal the Father to us because he had an intimate relationship with him. What characterized that relationship? Do you think it's possible for you to have that kind of relationship with the Father? Why or why not?

5. What is your response to the love Jesus has shown you on the cross? What more could you do to respond?

110

6. One Way

Are We Going in the Right Direction as a Disciple of Jesus?

All that we have looked at so far in *Rerouting* has been for the purpose of encountering Jesus. "Being Christian," Pope Benedict XVI was fond of saying, "is not the result of an ethical choice or a lofty idea, but the encounter with an event, a person, which gives life a new horizon and a decisive direction" (*Deus Caritas Est*, 1). Unfortunately, for many Catholics, such an encounter hasn't happened, at least not one that they can identify.

Objectively speaking, of course, each and every meeting with Jesus in the sacraments is an encounter of a supreme kind. But while this is true, the sacraments aren't magic. They presuppose faith. And many Catholics will openly tell you that, while they've grown up Catholic and received all their sacraments, they don't *know* Jesus; they don't have a living friendship with him. An alarming percentage of Catholics don't even know that they *can have* a friendship with Jesus. They've been, as it is often said today, "sacramentalized but not evangelized." Without this life-changing encounter, Catholics misunderstand the faith as a mere system of rules to follow or some sort of lifestyle choice.

But as crucial as this life-changing encounter is, it's only the first step.

Archbishop Vigneron is fond of using a triad to summarize our work in and for the new evangelization: "Encounter, Grow, and Witness." This chapter is all about that second word, *growing*. When Jesus breaks into our lives, one of his purposes is to call us to become his disciples—to follow him, to have our lives, under the power and influence of the Holy Spirit, come into ever greater conformity to his life.

Jesus does this because it is only to the degree we are conformed to him that we are authentically human. Or to put it in easier terms: the more we look like Jesus, the more fulfilled, the happier, we will be. This is because Jesus reveals not only who God is but who we are—or who we are called to be.

Before we move on, let's take a moment to ask ourselves: *What effect has my* Rerouting *journey had on me so far? Have I accepted the astonishing fact that God is passionately in love not just with us but* with me? *Am I left bewildered and amazed at the truth that the eternal Son of God is so in love with me that he has become the bridge to enable me to get home?*

If this is so for you, then you've made your U-turn, and you're heading in the right direction. If it's not, then I would beg you to not go any further yet but to stay in this place, lingering over all we have looked at so far, asking the Holy Spirit to "massage" these truths deeper and deeper into your mind and heart.

A helpful way to do this, I find, is to pray in front of a crucifix. When I pray before the crucifix, I can see, regardless of how I might feel, the love that God has for me. And I ask the Spirit to help me understand the cross, understand that this happened for me, and understand a bit better the love of God.

The next step: discipleship

Those of us who have at least begun to grasp the extraordinary truth of God's passionate love are ready for the next step. We're ready to grow. We're ready to look at our lives in light of the life of Jesus and to see where he is calling us to grow in greater conformity to him.

Perhaps the first question to ask ourselves is simply this: *Have I made a conscious decision to be his disciple?*

What does that practically mean? you might ask. Well, the most helpful passage I've ever found to answer that question is Mark 8:34. Jesus says to the crowds who are following him (that would be you and me right now), "If any man would come after me, let him deny himself and take up his cross and follow me."

Now, when I used to pray about that passage, the phrase that jumped out at me was "take up his cross." I know enough about the times in which Jesus lived to understand that these words weren't a mere image for his listeners. The men and women of Jesus' time regularly saw men crucified by the Romans in their towns and cities. It was the ultimate deterrent, the way in which the Romans kept their subjects in check. "Mess with us, and this will happen to you."

But as the years have gone by, as daunting as this part of the call to discipleship is, another phrase has troubled me even more. I used to think that when Jesus said his disciple had to "deny himself," it meant that we would have to embark on some penitential practices, like fasting or other efforts at self-denial. But this is not at all what he meant when he said those words. Scripture scholar Mary Healy states:

To **deny** . . . was a legal term signifying a complete disownment. It is easy to brush over Jesus' reference to *self*-denial—saying no to oneself—without fully appreciating what a radical notion it is. Most people recognize the value of occasional acts of moderation or self-restraint. But as the next phrase makes clear, Jesus is referring to a total shift of the center of gravity in one's life, a reckless abandonment to him that entails the letting go of all one's own attachments and agendas, even one's hold on life itself. (*The Gospel of Mark*, Catholic Commentary Series, 169)

So then, are we willing to surrender our lives to Jesus? This is the real question before us. All that the Lord has done for us in creating us, becoming man for us, becoming sin for us, going to the cross for us, rising from the dead for us, has been for *this*: to help us know that no one loves us as he does, that no one can be trusted as he can, and thus to surrender ourselves to him.

Living for another

So let's take a look at some concrete ways we can surrender to the Lord who has laid down his life for us.

We have to understand, first, that surrendering to Jesus is something we have to choose to do daily. I have a priest friend who was asked recently when he decided to become a priest. "This morning," he answered. In other words, while he might have been ordained twenty-some years ago, the decision to live as a priest is one that needs to be renewed daily.

The same is certainly true for marriage. And it's also true for the life of discipleship. Paul tells us in Romans to offer ourselves "as a living sacrifice" to God (12:1). This means that each day, I have to choose to crawl back on top of the altar.

Now, honestly, some days I really don't feel like getting back on that altar; some days I feel tired, worn out, selfish, and a host of other things. Many days I downright fall. A mentor of mine often said that the hardest thing you will ever do in your life is put your hands up and surrender to God. There's just so much in us that doesn't want to do this, doesn't want to relinquish the reins of our lives. We need to humbly acknowledge this and keep trying, asking for and trusting in God's mercy and his patience, asking for and trusting in his grace at work in our lives to keep going, to do the next right thing.

I was fortunate, when I was in the seminary in Rome, to live in the shadow of Pope St. John Paul II. Meeting him personally on a number of occasions, being present when he celebrated Mass, and listening to his general audiences in St. Peter's Square, are experiences that are difficult to put into words. Merely being in his presence was an overwhelming experience of being roused to surrender and authentic greatness. This was a man who was clearly "sold out" for Jesus, and he made it look attractive. In one of his letters, *On the Vocation and Mission of the Lay Faithful in the Church and in the World,* he reminds us:

> [T]he "good news" is directed to stirring a person to a conversion of heart and life and a clinging to Jesus Christ as Lord and Savior; to disposing a person to receive Baptism

and the Eucharist and to strengthen a person in the prospect and realization of new life according to the Spirit. (*Christifideles Laici*, 33)

The pope uses the term *conversion of heart*. Give some thought to that expression. How can it help us reflect a bit on surrender?

Well, that expression tells us that real conversion takes place in the heart—the deepest part of ourselves; that place where our feelings and thoughts, our desires and hopes, all come together. It's a place of great intensity, and there's nothing casual about it.

But conversion doesn't stay there. It gradually flows outward, affecting every area of a person's life. Think of a stone being dropped into the center of a pond, creating ripples that flow in concentric circles until the entire pond is affected. Conversion is like that; surrender is like that. It takes over more and more of a life, until it touches everything. And when I say that it touches everything, I mean *everything*.

A common misunderstanding in our modern culture is that faith is totally interior, belonging to the private realm of worship and feeling. That's another example of a "mutation." We want to see surrender and conversion not in their mutated forms but as they truly are.

Jesus reveals to us what a human life totally given over to God looks like. He didn't spend his life sitting on a mountaintop lost in prayer and contemplation. He lived his earthly life in the flesh. He healed people not just spiritually but of physical illnesses. He fed multitudes, not just by satisfying their spiritual hungers but by actually filling their stomachs.

He changed real water into real wine. He suffered greatly in the flesh. And he rose again, not as a disembodied spirit but in the flesh.

That shows us that we must transform not just our thoughts and feelings—our interior life—but our entire life. This encompasses the tangible as well as the intangible things: our relationships with others, our appetites for the things of this world, our desires for physical comfort, and a host of other things. As we surrender to God, we strive to bring "every thought captive to obey Christ" (2 Corinthians 10:5).

A real conversion involves letting things die within us. And here is one of the most profound paradoxes of the Christian life: Jesus tells us that "whoever would save his life will lose it; and whoever loses his life for my sake, he will save it" (Luke 9:24).

This dying, or losing our lives, takes many forms, at least in my life. I constantly run into obstacles—roadblocks that threaten to keep me from surrendering entirely to Jesus. I think most of us face more or less the same ones.

Number one among them, probably, is self-love. We might scoff at the ancients who bowed down to statues and idols, but all of us are idolatrous, in reality. And *the* idol for most of us is the idol of *self*.

At the heart of self-love is our desire to be our own god, to live for our own desires and pleasures. This is what Adam and Eve desired: to be autonomous, no longer dependent on God, even though they knew he was a good Father. Such self-love is self-destructive, because when we give in to it, we cut ourselves off from the source of life, God. The only proper response to this self-love, if we are to be not only disciples but also genuinely free men and women, is to put it to death.

This is a daunting task. Where does one begin? My guess is that most of us have a sense of where to start, even if we don't want to admit it. Let's face it: there are areas of our lives that are in darkness. We're painfully aware of some of those areas. Some are so shrouded in the shadows that we can't even name them. Perhaps there are secret places in us that we've never spoken about with anyone. Perhaps there are parts of us that we know are wrong but that seem essential to our very being. Maybe there are things in our past or present that we've never brought to the confessional. That might be the place for some of us to begin.

Jesus wants us to experience his healing and his power at work in our lives; he wants to free us from anything and everything that makes us feel "stuck." He wants us to begin again. We may need to ask for courage to confess our most secret sins and allow Jesus to uproot them. When we let the light of Christ do its work in the dark places of our souls, we can reorient our lives, bringing "every thought captive to obey Christ."

Let's go back to those words of Jesus in Mark 8:34, which we looked at earlier in this chapter: "If any man would come after me, let him deny himself and take up his cross and follow me." Let's ask ourselves a frank question.

Who owns me?

Jesus tells us that if we decide to come after him, we need to "deny" ourselves. To "deny" ourselves does not mean to do acts of penance but to renounce ownership of our lives and give all to Jesus. When I think about this, I picture signing over the deed of my life to Jesus. In fact, on countless occasions, I have written in my prayer journal, "Today, [whatever the date is], I, John, sign over the rights of my life to Jesus."

As we noted earlier, true conversion—real surrender—must affect every area of our lives. Well then, conversion and surrender must also involve an acknowledgement that every area of our lives is ultimately *owned* by Jesus. And *that* is a hard thing for men and women to acknowledge.

Owned? You must be kidding! No one *owns* me. Does God want me to be some sort of slave who asks, "How high?" whenever he says, "Jump"?

Hardly. I know this because God has himself *become a slave* for me (see Philippians 2:7). He's not interested in taking away my freedom; he wants me to truly *be free*. But again, here's the paradox: real freedom comes from letting Jesus have the reins to every area of my life.

I once heard a priest say, "If Jesus is not Lord of your body, your time, and your money, then what in the world is he Lord of?" *My body, my time, and my money.* Those three areas of our lives are perhaps the ones where we should all start as we examine the question, "Who owns me?"

My body

St. Paul writes, "Do you not know that your body is a temple of the Holy Spirit within you, which you have from God? You are not your own; you were bought with a price. So glorify God in your body" (1 Corinthians 6:19-20).

These are incredible words to pray and meditate on. I am not my own. My body was given to me once, when God created me; then given back to me a second time, when Jesus redeemed me by his passion; and given to me a third time, if you will, when the Holy Spirit began to dwell in me by baptism. I truly am not my own. Everything is gift—a gift from a generous, loving, saving, freeing, redeeming, bleeding God!

Our modern culture assaults us with slogans like "My body, my choice!" But the truth is that it is *not* "my body." I didn't create myself. I received my life. It was and is a gift. And the Giver of this gift is to be trusted.

Who is more deserving of trust than Jesus? Who has done for us anything that can remotely compare to what Jesus has done for us? He is the one through whom I was made, and he has become man for me and laid down his life for me. He has proven his love as has no other.

And this Jesus, who can be trusted as no other, who has proven his love by going to the cross for me, speaks to me quite frankly about the body and about sexuality. He tells me, for example, that lust is not some harmless thing that hurts no one but rather is destructive, because lust reduces another person to a mere object for my own enjoyment. And we all know, deep down at least, that real men and real women don't treat others as mere objects. Persons aren't things. Every human person is created in the image and likeness of God. Every person deserves to be loved and cherished, not objectified.

Now, lust isn't the same thing as attraction. It is healthy to be attracted to people. (God, after all, is attracted to us!) There's nothing wrong with that. But attraction doesn't objectify the other. It sees the beauty of the other, both interior and exterior.

Is Jesus really Lord of my body and especially of my attitudes toward sex? In a world corrupted by lust (see 2 Peter 1:4)—and we could say, saturated with pornography— am I striving to let him have the reins of my thoughts and behaviors?

Yes, we might struggle in this area. But do we at least *want* to want to let him be Lord? For some of us, that is the place to start.

My time

God has allotted me a certain number of years, days, minutes, and seconds on earth. That time is mine, yet it is not mine. It belongs ultimately to the one who gave it to me, and he gave it to me to use, not to fritter away.

There are certain things that I must do with my time if I want to give my life to Jesus. One of these is regular participation in the Eucharistic liturgy. The Mass is not just the "source and summit" of our faith; it is the most intimate communion possible with Jesus, the one who wants to draw us into his own divine life. If I cannot find the time for this, for what can I find time?

So I must always be sure to give the Eucharistic celebration adequate time. But let's be clear about what that means. It certainly means more than grudgingly showing up for one hour each week and daydreaming that hour away. It means trying to pray with the readings in advance. It means coming as an active participant rather than as a silent spectator. It means not simply listening to the prayers but doing my best to enter into them, even when it is done silently. It means being as totally present as possible during the time that I am at Mass. It means participating with my whole being.

Jesus is literally giving himself to me in the Mass—his body, blood, soul, and divinity. He's holding nothing back! It is only right that I give myself to him at the same moment. What does it say about me if I don't even try?

But giving Jesus ownership over my time isn't restricted to Sundays. If I am to have a friendship with God, I need to set aside time for daily prayer. There's no other way to have a friendship with someone than to spend time with him, talking and listening to him.

Remember the story of the Samaritan woman at the well in the Gospel of St. John? Jesus, tired and thirsty, says to the woman, "Give me a drink" (4:7). He asks for a drink in another place in Scripture. Do you remember it? It's also in the Gospel of St. John, but this time in the passion narrative. "I thirst," Jesus says as he hangs on the cross (19:28). Why does he say that? For what is Jesus thirsting?

The answer is: for you—and for me. God *thirsts* for us. Mother Teresa used to remind her sisters that to say "I thirst," means more than to say "I love you." It means more like, "I want you; I desire you!" This is the gospel! The God who is infinitely happy and lacking in nothing *wants* you.

When we go to pray, his thirst for us meets our thirst for him, even when we do not realize that we are thirsting for him. Our prayer can quench that burning thirst of his. Our prayer is a demonstration of the love that Jesus wants to receive from us. Prayer should permeate our days and nights, like the air we breathe. It should fill our time in a way that nothing else does or can.

Is time before the Blessed Sacrament a regular part of your life? I don't know a better habit to acquire and to work on than spending a holy hour every day before Jesus. Nothing has changed my life as this has. Bishop Fulton Sheen used to say that just as our skin changes by being exposed to the heat of the sun, so our souls are changed by being exposed to the Son.

Now, some of us, for a host of reasons, are not able to get to a church or chapel for a holy hour every day. That's okay. We can still set aside some time each day to be with Jesus. Whatever amount of time that is, know that God delights to meet you in prayer, where his thirst and yours encounter each other.

Another great habit is the regular reading of Scripture. I don't know the precise numbers, but I'm sure that years of our lives are given over to satisfying our need for food and drink. But those aren't our only needs. The Bible tells us that there is a famine in the land, not for food but for the word of God (see Amos 8:11).

Each and every day, we put into our ears and eyes and minds words from the world around us. This is a good thing to do: we need to know what's going on. We have a desire to know, a desire that is a gift from God. We can and want to understand things. But nothing can teach me about life as Scripture can.

Scripture is not the words of men but the word of God; it is revelation. In it I find the answers to life's crucial questions. And perhaps, most importantly, if I do not read the Bible, and especially the gospels, I will make up my own version and idea of God and of Jesus. And whatever idea or version I come up with, it won't be accurate. I can only know God if he reveals himself to me, and he does that in an absolutely unique way in Scripture.

Getting to Confession regularly is another great use of our time. Personally, at one point in my life, I hadn't gone to Confession for almost ten years. Now I go at least every other week. The sad truth, according to virtually every study done on the Church today, is that most Catholics never go to Confession, and many Catholics go very infrequently. I didn't go all those years because I was both proud and afraid.

But there's nothing at all to be afraid of! God loves to forgive! And the Scriptures remind us again and again that God loves the humble. So even if it's been decades since your last confession, come back! Don't be afraid. The priest won't yell at you for having been away so long. He will be the expression of the Father's merciful love.

And you will be able to begin again. You will, we could say, get your life back, and what a glorious thing that is! I can honestly tell you that hearing even one confession of a person who has been away from God and is returning makes my whole life worth living.

The true disciple is deliberate and intentional in making time to go to Mass, pray, read Scripture, and celebrate the Sacrament of Confession. Is that what you do? If not, why not start tomorrow—or even today?

But not only should we spend time on these things; we should let the Lord permeate every dimension of our lives, to truly be Lord of all our time, not just the time we spend doing "holy things." That doesn't mean we can't go on vacation, play cards, go golfing, go out to eat, or have fun. Hardly! Jesus lived in a time when people ate three-hour meals! His first miracle involved 180 gallons of wine! God, I would argue, loves to play, and he calls us to enter into his own joy.

But we want to do everything in such a way that we can look back on the day and thank God sincerely for everything. I find myself asking Jesus over and over again, "Teach me, Lord, how to be a man. Teach me how to work, how to play, how to rest, how to eat, how to pray, how to enjoy friendship. Help me be ever more human."

My money

Finally, let's look at money. Ouch!

Our money is like our time and our body: it belongs, really, to God. We are all stewards, and a steward is entrusted with something that belongs to another. What do we have that belongs to another? How about everything? "Name something you have that you have not received," Paul says (cf. 1 Corinthians 4:7).

The person striving to be a disciple of Jesus, to be truly free and authentically human, should give their "first fruits" directly to the Lord before allocating money for anything else. I know that's hard to hear, but it's true. The biblical standard of the tithe is very relevant here. The tithe consists of 10 percent of one's income, which is given back to the Lord. The experience of countless generations is that when we are generous with the Lord— when we give him the first fruits of our income rather than the leftovers—his generosity in return is without compare.

Now, that doesn't mean that we should give so that we will get back, as if this is some sort of magic formula. But when we are generous to the Lord, we do release tremendous blessing, providence, and mercy in our lives.

I was blessed to have a dad who modeled this for my siblings and me. He gave a ridiculous amount of his income—at least that's what I thought when I was young. He did it all with great joy. He knew that God had put into his hands the resources he had, and it was a true blessing for him to be able to share them with others.

Tithing can work in many ways. For example, it can be split. Archbishop Vigneron refers to a "5-4-1" formula. Five percent goes to the parish, 4 percent goes to charities of our choice, and 1 percent goes to the various needs of the archdiocese.

However we may choose to give, the simple truth is that you and I are created in the image and likeness of God, and God *gives*. The Trinity, as we saw earlier, is a kind of reckless exchange of love, holding nothing back from the other. This is why happiness comes from giving—not just our money or our time—but ourselves. When we make of ourselves a genuine gift to another, we are living as God does, and God is the happiest of all beings.

The fruits of discipleship

What do I get out of all this? Perhaps that's a question that's going through your mind right now. Or maybe I'm just more selfish than most people or more honest, because I think of that question all the time, or at least I used to. After all, this isn't some small thing that's being asked of me. God is asking for it all!

For what it's worth, even St. Peter asked, "What's in it for me?" In Mark's Gospel, just after Jesus spoke about the dangers of riches and how hard it is for a rich person to enter into the kingdom of God, Peter said to Jesus, "Lo, we have left everything and followed you" (10:28). In other words, *What are we going to get?*

And the answer is "more." Jesus tells Peter (and each of us):

Truly, I say to you, there is no one who has left house or brothers or sisters or mother or father or children or lands, for my sake and for the gospel, who will not receive a hundredfold now in this time, houses and brothers and sisters and mothers and children and lands, with persecutions, and in the age to come eternal life. (Mark 10:29-30)

The God who is Love and is the Creator of everything that is offers us eternal life. *Eternal* doesn't simply mean "unending." In fact, unending life wouldn't necessarily be a gift at all. Pope Benedict XVI, in a letter on hope, wrote:

To continue living for ever—endlessly—appears more like a curse than a gift. Death, admittedly, one would wish to postpone for as long as possible. But to live always, without end—this, all things considered, can only be monotonous and ultimately unbearable. This is precisely the point made, for example, by Saint Ambrose, one of the Church Fathers, in the funeral discourse for his deceased brother Satyrus:

"Death was not part of nature; it became part of nature. God did not decree death from the beginning; he prescribed it as a remedy. Human life, because of sin, . . . began to experience the burden of wretchedness in unremitting labor and unbearable sorrow. There had to be a limit to its evils; death had to restore what life had forfeited. Without the assistance of grace, immortality is more of a burden than a blessing." (*Spe Salvi*, 10, quoting *De excessu fratris sui Satyri*, II, 47)

But eternal life isn't simply unending life; it is the fullness of life. It is true life, abundant life. In that same letter, Pope Benedict wrote:

Saint Augustine, in the extended letter on prayer which he addressed to Proba, a wealthy Roman widow and mother of three consuls, once wrote this: ultimately we want only one thing—"the blessed life," the life which is simply life, simply "happiness." In the final analysis, there is nothing else that we ask for in prayer. Our journey has no other goal—it is about this alone. But then Augustine also says: looking more closely, we have no idea what we ultimately desire, what we would really like. We do not know this reality at all; even in those moments when we think we can reach out and touch it, it eludes us. . . . All we know is that it is not this. (*Spe Salvi*, 11, citing *Ad Probam* 14, 25-15)

Finally the pope wrote:

[*Eternal life*] is an inadequate term that creates confusion. "Eternal," in fact, suggests to us the idea of something interminable, and this frightens us; "life" makes us think of the life that we know and love and do not want to lose, even though very often it brings more toil than satisfaction, so that while on the one hand we desire it, on the other hand we do not want it. To imagine ourselves outside the temporality that imprisons us and in some way to sense that eternity is not an unending succession of days in the calendar, but something more like the supreme moment of satisfaction, in which totality embraces us and we embrace totality—this we can only attempt. It would be like plunging into the ocean of infinite love, a moment in which time—the before and after—no longer exists. We can only attempt to grasp the idea that such a moment is life in the full sense, a plunging ever anew into the vastness of being, in which we are simply overwhelmed with joy. (*Spe Salvi*, 12)

What do we get out of following Jesus? Overwhelmed by joy, plunged into an ocean of infinite love. Sign me up!

So we've made our U-turn. We're on a brand-new road, and it's heading toward Jesus. But we still have our work cut out for us. We have the basic tools we need to begin that wonderful process of surrender to Jesus—to the one who loves us beyond all our imagining. So begin it or continue it. Surrender yourself more and more every day, until you become the disciple you were created to be, until you can say with St. Paul, "It is no longer I who live, but Christ who lives in me" (Galatians 2:20).

Questions for Reflection and Discussion

1. Have you signed over "the deed" of your life to Jesus? If not, what is holding you back?

2. How can you allow Jesus' light to shine in the dark areas of your life? What prevents you from coming to him for forgiveness? How can you overcome these obstacles when you face them?

3. Is Jesus truly the Lord of your body and your sexuality? Regardless of how you may struggle in this area, do you want to let the Lord truly reign in your body? If not, why not?

4. How do you allocate your time? Does the use of your time show you're living less and less for yourself and more and more for Christ and others? Where could you make better use of the time God gives you each day?

5. Do you see your possessions as your own or on loan from God? How might he be calling you to give more of your treasure to build his kingdom?

7. Enter Here

We Can Listen to Jesus' Voice Calling Us to Surrender to Him

If we are going to become disciples of Jesus, we need to learn how to recognize his voice. Our relationship with the Lord can only grow if we listen carefully to what he has to say to us. He speaks to us so that he can guide us, comfort us, convict us, and show us how much we are loved. He speaks to us so that we might find the happiness for which he has created us.

It's very important that we learn to distinguish his voice from other voices—voices that might prevent us from fully surrendering our lives to God. These voices, like a road sign, warn, "Do not enter!"

"My sheep hear my voice" (John 10:27), Jesus assures us. And we can conclude from his words that he knows exactly how to talk to us—to each one of us in all our individuality. The problem is that we may not know how to listen.

So let's try to learn how to listen. In fact, let's make that our goal for this chapter: learning to discern the voice of God. What does "God's voice" mean exactly? Is recognizing it more easily said than done?

Do you think you've ever heard God's voice? I mean, really heard it? If so, what was it like? You probably didn't hear it in the same way you hear the voices of people around you. God's voice is usually different. It's usually without sound, without words—a silent voice that has been heard by countless people over the centuries. And it's a voice more powerful than any other.

A voice without sound, without words: Is that some kind of contradiction in terms? No. It may seem to be, but it's not.

Discerning God's voice

As we try to discern, one of the first things we have to do—and probably one of the hardest—is to give God time to speak. Expecting God to respond the way people do to your text messages is a recipe for frustration. So don't do it! God isn't bound to any schedule we devise. All time is God's time, and he will use it as he chooses.

In other words, there's no way to hurry God along. On the other hand, there's certainly no way to hold him back once he's chosen the perfect moment to speak to you. And the moment will be perfect, even if from your standpoint it may not seem to be. In fact, God's voice may seem to come at the worst possible moment: years too late or way too early. But from the standpoint of eternity, God will speak to you at precisely—and I really do mean *precisely*—the right moment.

Now let's try to think of the means through which God speaks to us. Often God's voice comes to us through encounters we have with others. Sometimes it comes in prayer. Occasionally it might take the form of a sudden awareness of something we hadn't thought of before. It may come while we're reading Scripture.

The problem is that these things can all be confusing. They can cause more uncertainty than certainty. When we are in the midst of them, we may not be sure how to distinguish the voice of God from the voice of the world around us, the voices in our own minds, and especially the voices of fallen angels who are intent on our destruction.

Distinguishing God's voice may seem difficult, but it's not impossible—at least it's not for a Catholic who knows something about the faith and has tried to live it. In fact, I believe we can apply a simple and straightforward standard: if what we believe to be the voice of God is in sync with what has been revealed in the Scriptures and the teachings of the Church, then there's a good chance it's from God. If it is not in sync, there's no chance that it's from God.

I know that many of the things I hear—or think I hear—are pretty clearly not from God. But I believe some of the things are. And over the years, I've learned how God usually chooses to speak to me. Unsurprisingly, he does it by using something that is already part of me.

I am a very visual person. I have a vivid imagination, and I easily and often picture things in my mind. And God speaks to me often through images. I want to share one of those images with you now.

It occurred at a funeral at which I officiated. The funeral was for a person who was, by all accounts, a truly good man. Married to his wife for forty years, he was the father of six children. For at least thirty years, he was a daily communicant. For a good long time, he was intentional and deliberate in trying to make his family and friends aware of the difference that Jesus made in his life. And if you remember the previous chapter, you'll know that what he was doing is one of the marks of a real disciple.

Now, please understand that I don't want to canonize this man. I'll let God handle that. However, I am saying that he loved God deeply and he loved his neighbor. And that's a lot. In fact, it's exactly what Jesus reduces the Ten Commandments to in the gospels:

> And one of the scribes came up and . . . asked him, "Which commandment is the first of all?" Jesus answered, "The first is, 'Hear, O Israel: The Lord our God, the Lord is one; and you shall love the Lord your God with all your heart, and with all your soul, and with all your mind, and with all your strength.' The second is this, 'You shall love your neighbor as yourself.' There is no other commandment greater than these." (Mark 12:28-31)

So the man we were burying had lived a life that fulfills the greatest of God's commandments. Not bad. Who among us can say the same?

After we had blessed the body at the entrance of the church, we were slowly processing to the front. As we did this, I saw something remarkable in my mind. I saw a crowd stand and begin to applaud, and it wasn't polite or reserved applause. This applause was loud, energetic, and filled with emotion. Actually, what I saw was like a tunnel, the kind that football players run through on their way into the stadium. And just like at a football game, the crowd was pounding on top of the tunnel as the players ran through. But in this case, there was only one man who ran through, the man we were burying.

I know that sounds pretty fanciful. But I don't really think it is. In fact, I think it's very much in line with Scripture. Let's take a look at the Letter to the Hebrews:

Therefore, since we are surrounded by so great a cloud of witnesses, let us also lay aside every weight, and sin which clings so closely, and let us run with perseverance the race that is set before us, looking to Jesus the pioneer and perfecter of our faith, who for the joy that was set before him endured the cross, despising the shame, and is seated at the right hand of the throne of God. (12:1-2)

That passage follows immediately after what is commonly referred to as the "Hall of Faith." It's essentially a listing of the great saints of the Old Testament, a wondrously diverse group of people. It enumerates the ways in which they persevered, the great things they accomplished. After describing them, the Letter to the Hebrews arrives at the above passage, which paints a picture of heaven as being something like a stadium that's packed with people. All those people are saints.

If the saints are in the stadium, where are we? We're on the field, running the race, playing the game that is called life.

A cheering section

Let me share another image with you. I'd like to do so especially for those who might be putting off making a commitment to Jesus out of some kind of fear. It happened to me about seven years ago, on a Saturday night in November.

I had just come home after celebrating Mass, and it was one of those rare nights for me when I had nothing on my calendar. So I cooked up a pound of pasta and headed down to my basement to watch some college football. I switched on the TV, and it was the Nebraska versus Texas A&M game, taking place in College Station, Texas.

If you know anything about Texas A&M, you're aware that the stadium, Kyle Field, is called "the twelfth man." A football team consists of eleven men. The crowd at Texas A&M is considered an extra player, a virtual participant in the game. Why?

Because Texas A&M's crowd is loud! I mean, really loud! Students are more or less forbidden to sit during home games. And they don't have cheerleaders. They have "yell leaders," a group of five upperclassmen who whip the crowd into a frenzy. Kyle Field seats just under 103,000 people. At this particular game, everyone was dressed in white; they call such games "white outs."

I was sitting there, pasta in hand, watching the pregame, and already the crowd was amped up, bouncing up and down. In fact, the upper deck of the stadium actually looked as if *it* was bouncing. Then, out of nowhere, I heard the Lord say to me, "That's heaven." And he took me to the eleventh chapter of the Letter to the Hebrews, that hall of faith in which so many of our ancestors in faith are listed.

Now, understand, the fans at Kyle Stadium, and at so many other stadiums across the country, don't go to a football game to *watch* it. They go to change the outcome! They go to inspire eleven men on the field to do things that they could never do in their backyard, in front of Mom and Dad and a few friends. And that's what the saints do for us. They're not sitting in the bleachers, looking down and saying anything like, "It looks nasty down there. I'm glad I'm done with all that. Good luck!" No! They're on their feet cheering for us, praying for us, urging us on.

How do we know that? Because we know the great commandment. It's not just we here on earth who follow the great commandment; so do the saints. They too love God and their neighbor. And who are the saints' neighbors? We are! And because we are their neighbors, they pray for us.

Nobody in heaven needs prayer. They're already home, enjoying that perfect happiness we were all created for. They don't have to pray for each other, but they do pray for us—the ones on earth who are still playing the game of life.

What does that mean? It means that right now, in heaven, you and I have family and friends and untold numbers of other people who are on their feet cheering for us, praying for us, urging us on with every fiber of their being.

No one size fits all saints

Let's turn our attention back to the man whose funeral I spoke of. But keep that "cloud of witnesses" and the image of the stadium in mind. You'll need them.

Remember that the man was outspoken in sharing his faith. Remember as well that he was a daily communicant for over thirty years. Now try to imagine him—what he was like, what he did for a living. Maybe you think he was a deacon or someone involved with some kind of Church work. He wasn't. He was a coach in the National Football League. He coached some of the greatest players who have ever played the game. And that means he's probably not the sort of person you think of when you try to conjure up an image of a man who has done his best to give ownership of his life to Jesus.

And that's exactly the point.

We've all seen the road sign, "Do Not Enter." That refers to a fear that is rampant in many of us. The fear can be expressed like this: "Do not enter! If you really commit to Jesus, you're going to have to give up all your individuality and probably just about everything you love. You're going to become like 'them,' a bunch of clones and maybe even clowns."

Rubbish! The man I've just been speaking of made that commitment, and it didn't diminish his life. It enhanced it!

Let's look at the saints—the great cloud of witnesses—and see who some of them actually are. Yes, there are some bishops and priests and deacons and religious. But there are also husbands and wives, like Louis and Zélie Martin, the parents of St. Thérèse. There are single people, like Pier Giorgio Frassati. There are repentant murderers, like Alessandro Serenelli. There are kings, like Louis of France and Stephen of Hungary. There are philosophers, like Thomas Aquinas. There are former atheists, like Edith Stein. There are doctors, like Gianna Molla, lawyers, like Thomas More, and scientists, like Jérôme Lejeune. There are very young people, like Kizito of Uganda and Antonietta Meo, who may become the youngest person ever recognized as "Venerable" and who suffered greatly from cancer. And there are elderly people, like Mother Teresa of Calcutta, who spent her long life caring for others.

In heaven there are athletes, coaches, and CEOs. There are people with interests and loves that are indistinguishable from the interests and loves of people you know. And that should make us understand that heaven isn't a one-size-fits-all place.

The one thing that all the saints have in common is that, sooner or later, they all had a life-changing encounter with Jesus and surrendered to him. They all said, "Lord, I will do whatever you want." That's it.

Don't be afraid to enter

Like many of you, I've known God since I was a child. I've prayed for as long as I can remember. But please don't take that to mean that I have always walked faithfully as a Christian. Like so many people, I very deliberately put off making the decision to follow Jesus because I was deathly afraid of what would happen to me if I did that. Does that sound familiar?

There was a voice in my head—and I think that same voice is in the heads of many people. It said over and over again, "Do not enter! If you enter and surrender to Jesus, you will lose your identity and all the things you love." It said, "Do not enter! If you do, you'll lose control of your life." It said, "Do not enter! The Christian life is less, not more. If you give yourself to Jesus, you'll probably never have any fun again." It said, "Do not enter! If you do, you'll become some sort of Jesus freak." It said, "Do not enter! If you do, God's going to make you do things you don't want to do—things that you hate. It's just going to be too hard."

And then the voice took another approach—a far more devastating one. It said, "Do not enter! You're not good enough—not with all the things you've done in your life." It said, "Do not enter! The Church is a place for super Catholics, the spiritual elite, the ones who have it all together. Who do you think *you* are, comparing yourself to them?"

Let's deal with the last objection first. And we'll do that by telling a universal truth.

The Church does not exist for a spiritual elite, because there is no spiritual elite. We're all human, all affected by original sin, and all our lives are disordered in one way or another. No priest has it together, and neither does any member of a religious community.

I've been a priest for more than twenty years now, and I've heard thousands of confessions. I can assure you that we are all sinners. We're all works in progress. We're all struggling with something.

Your parish is not a meeting place for the perfected. It's a place for anyone who wants to encounter Jesus. It's for those who are hungry for more. It's for those who want more than what the world can offer, those looking for real depth in their lives. It's for those who suspect that Jesus was telling the truth when he said, "I came that they may have life, and have it abundantly" (John 10:10).

I don't know about you, but I want more. If there's abundant life to be had, then I want it! I've tried almost everything the world can offer, and it's not enough. I have a bigger appetite than this world can satisfy. There's a hole inside me that can't be filled by anything but God, and that aches when it's empty.

And after looking at all that Jesus has done for us, as we have in the previous chapters, I believe I can trust him. I believe that all of us can trust him. I believe that all of us *must* trust him.

Let's look at the life of St. Augustine, who lived hundreds of years ago. He was hungry for truth; he was hungry for goodness; he was hungry for beauty. And that's not all he was hungry for. Augustine's physical appetites were substantial, and he lived a very disordered life because of them. He yearned to become a Christian, but one massive obstacle stood in his path: chastity seemed impossible for him.

Then one day Augustine experienced a vision of a host of saints, young and old, male and female. And all of them had made the decision to turn around, reroute their lives, and surrender to God. All of them had embraced the chastity that Augustine thought he could not.

"Can you not do what these men have done, what these women have done?" the voice of a beautiful woman he called "Continence" seemed to be saying to him. It was as if the holy men and women in his vision were cheering him on, praying for him.

Shortly afterward Augustine heard a child's voice urging him to pick up the Bible and read. He picked it up, and these were the words to which he opened: "Put on the Lord Jesus Christ, and make no provision for the flesh" (Romans 13:14).

At that moment, Augustine surrendered his life to Jesus (*Confessions*, book 8, chapters 11 and 12). He took his first step on the path that would lead him to become not only one of the greatest theologians in the history of the Church but one of the most significant figures in human history.

This last story is far more personal. It happened at my mother's kitchen table. The two of us were talking, drifting from one topic to another. The conversation eventually turned to my father and my brother, both of whom we had lost in the previous year.

As we spoke, my eyes were drawn to a photograph on the table, one that I had never seen before. There were my dad and my brother, sitting in Comerica Park, home of the Detroit Tigers. I never even knew that the two of them had gone to a game together without anyone else from the family. But there they were, in the order in which they had left us. And they were staring out from the picture. It was as if they were looking directly at me. And for a moment, as I held that photo, it felt as if they were speaking to me, saying something like, "Come on, John! You can do this! Take the final steps; surrender yourself to Jesus. Come on, John! Just give it all to Jesus."

What do I conclude from that? Two things. The first is that God is constantly speaking to us—speaking to us through the most ordinary things of our lives—and that what he says to us is of vital importance.

The second thing is that I have—you have—family and friends in heaven right now. And they aren't simply watching us. They're cheering for us, rooting us on as we make our journey through life. They're praying for us, doing everything they can for us, so that we can run the race, fight the fight. They are loving us with a love that we can barely comprehend, so that one day we will join them in a place that is beyond all description, a place where we finally experience the fulfillment of all desire.

There is nothing more important than giving everything to God, and we are indeed surrounded by a great cloud of witnesses who will help us do that. So don't be afraid. Don't pay any attention to those voices that tell you, "Do not enter." Don't even glance in their direction. Pay attention instead to the voice—that quiet but incessant voice—that calls to you from every corner of your life.

"My sheep hear my voice," Jesus tells us. And we *will* hear his voice if we try to. He speaks to us constantly, and what he is says is "Enter." He stands on the other side of the door that is our minds and our hearts. He is waiting for us to fall into his embrace the moment we throw that door open.

So do what the one who loves you more than anyone else wants you to do. Listen to his voice. Open that door that you've kept so tightly closed, and enter. Simply enter.

You can count on Jesus to do the rest.

Questions for Reflection and Discussion

1. There are voices in everyone's life that tell them, "Do not enter." What voices say that to you? What can you do to hear God's welcoming voice more clearly?

2. Have you ever thought that God was speaking to you? What did it feel like? How was it different from the many voices that you hear in our busy and noisy world?

3. What are the means through which you would expect God to speak to you? Are they visual, emotional, liturgical, or scriptural? Why do you think God would use these means? What do they say about you?

4. A "great cloud of witnesses" is praying for you and cheering you on. What role do the saints play in your life? Do you have devotion to any specific saint?

5. Why do you think we often harbor fears that our lives will be diminished in some way if we surrender to Jesus? How can you grow in trust that Jesus will give you what truly satisfies?

Go!

*And Jesus came and said to them, "All authority in heaven
and on earth has been given to me. Go therefore and make
disciples of all nations, baptizing them in the name of the
Father and of the Son and of the Holy Spirit, teaching
them to observe all that I have commanded you; and
behold, I am with you always, to the close of the age."
(Matthew 28:18-20)*

*And he said to them, "Go into all the world
and preach the gospel to the whole creation."
(Mark 16:15)*

*Woe to me if I do not preach the gospel!
(1 Corinthians 9:16)*

*Knowing Jesus is the best gift that any person can receive;
that we have encountered him is the best thing that
has happened in our lives; and making him known by
our word and deeds is our joy.
(Latin American and Caribbean Bishops,
Aparecida Document, 2007)*

So here we are at the end of this little book. But it's not an end
at all. Everything up to this point has been for *this* moment.
Or as a friend of mine in the parish often says, "So what?
Now what?" Indeed, now what?

I mentioned earlier that my archbishop, Allen Vigneron, frequently repeats the triad "Encounter, Grow, Witness" as a summary of our call to the new evangelization. Perhaps we could reword it: "Encounter, Grow, Go!" We want to offer every person in our community a life-changing encounter with Jesus.

And Jesus doesn't just want us to *meet* him; he wants us to grow in real intimacy with him. He is the best and most faithful of friends, a friend who proves his love by laying down his life for us. He wants us to grow in conformity with him who alone is "the way, and the truth, and the life" (John 14:6).

But even this is not enough; it's not the end. We have been called into trinitarian friendship and given the power of the Holy Spirit, not just for our own sakes but so that we can go out into the world and tell others of the God who would rather die than live without us. We—all of us!—are invited and charged to be heralds of the good news that the good Father is passionately in love with his creation; that his Son entered into the muck of human existence, taking upon himself our sins and rescuing us from the clutches of death, hell, and Satan—all so that we could share in his divine life for all eternity.

In my personal experience and in my experience walking with other Catholics for many years, this last part, "Witness" or "Go," seems to be the hardest to put into practice. For many, the pinnacle of the Christian life is "living a holy life." This is typically understood as reordering, or rerouting, the direction of our lives toward Jesus and rooting out grave sin. Such a person is faithful to daily prayer, reads the Bible, gets to Mass every Sunday and perhaps other days during the week, regularly goes to Confession, and even helps out in the parish. These folks are disciples of Jesus, living faithful lives, orienting their time, money, and life around him. This is great—praise God!

But as great as it is, Jesus calls us to more. "God wants his world back," Archbishop Vigneron often says, and it's our great joy and privilege to help bring this about. This happens by our being intentional and deliberate in telling others about Jesus. Curtis Martin, the founder of FOCUS (Fellowship of Catholic University Students), frequently says that God doesn't call us just to be *faithful* but to be *fruitful*. I can't tell you how much this simple statement has convicted me the past few years.

The Great Commission, found at the conclusion of the Gospels of Matthew and Mark, makes this clear. "Go!" Jesus says. Where? "Into all the world." And to whom does he say this? To all of us.

By all means, we should strive to cooperate with the Holy Spirit in bringing our lives into greater and greater conformity to Jesus. But the Spirit wants to send us out. He wants to put into us that same passion that consumed Paul, who said to the church in Corinth, "Woe to me if I do not preach the gospel!" (1 Corinthians 9:16).

Paul was inflamed with love for both God and those around him who were lost in the darkness that is life apart from God. And so he went out, he spoke, he bore witness to Jesus. *This was what he lived for.* Like the bishops in Latin America, he would say, "Knowing Jesus is the best gift that any person can receive; that we have encountered him is the best thing that has happened in our lives; and making him known by our word and deeds is our joy."

The fruit of love

Jesus prays in the Gospel of John that we, his disciples, would "bear much fruit" (15:8). In fact, he alludes to bearing fruit at least six times in the first eight verses of chapter 15. What fruit is he looking for? Well, to be sure, he's looking for the fruit of love to take root in our lives. This love can and should be manifested in a variety of ways.

For example, Jesus speaks at the end of Matthew 25 about the need—the demand—to feed the hungry, give drink to the thirsty, clothe the naked, visit the sick and the imprisoned, and welcome the stranger. These are concrete ways we can and must love if we are to be his disciples and to be welcomed one day into his Father's kingdom. We must take these words very seriously! Where we are going to spend eternity depends on them.

And at the end of the day, what is more loving than to rescue someone from the hunger, the thirst, the loneliness, and the sickness that is life apart from God? What is more loving than to introduce to Jesus someone who does not know him?

This world and its amusements and distractions cannot quench the hunger and the thirst that lie at the deepest center of every human person. This is because, as St. Augustine famously said, "You have made us for yourself, O Lord, and our hearts are restless until they rest in you" (*Confessions*, book 1, 1).

In other words, God has made us *ordered* to himself. We are created to know him and his profound, personal, and extraordinary love. And while many of us spend years and years, and gobs of money along the way, trying to satisfy our desire for happiness, only God can fill that hole. This isn't true for *some* of us; it's true for *all* of us. There isn't a *single* person on the face of the earth who hasn't been made to share in God's own life for all eternity.

"This generation of Christians is responsible for this generation." I heard these words quoted by Curtis Martin at a FOCUS conference a few years back. Hear that again, please: "This generation of Christians is responsible for this generation." You and I are responsible for those around us who do not know Jesus. You are responsible for those around you who do not know Jesus. I am responsible for those around me who do not know Jesus. There is no "Plan B." God has not entrusted the gospel to angels; he has entrusted it to us. There is no cavalry coming; it's just us.

But we're not alone. We have each other, and we are filled with the power of the Holy Spirit, that same Holy Spirit who raised Jesus from the dead. What a joy! What a privilege! What an honor!

Yes, we won't always be well received. But who cares? We are disciples of a crucified Lord, after all. How can we hold this truth in? How can we keep this good news to ourselves?

As we close this book, let's ask the Lord these simple question: "With whom are you calling me to share the gospel, Jesus? Whom are you asking me to befriend, to walk with, to accompany, to invest in? Can I bring 'one more' to you?" And then let's GO!

THE REROUTING RESPONSE PLEDGE

More than forty-one hundred people have signed this card, including some from around the world who have heard our *Rerouting* program online. Pray about whether you are ready to make this pledge.

My Response: Living My Life for Jesus

I, _____, a repentant sinner, decide today, _____, to surrender the ownership of my life to the good Father. I renew the vows of my baptism to renounce Satan and to follow Jesus Christ more deliberately than I ever have before. Jesus, I give you my heart, that you may forever set it on fire for love of you and for others. Keep my heart pure with your perfect love, so that I may entrust myself totally to you. Jesus, please use me, that I might bring "one more" to you.

God the Father

_____   _____
Witness   My Signature

The complete *Rerouting* program is available for viewing online at https://www.olgcparish.net/rerouting/.

Thisbook was published by The Word Among Us. Since 1981, The Word Among Us has been answering the call of the Second Vatican Council to help Catholic laypeople encounter Christ in the Scriptures.

The name of our company comes from the prologue to the Gospel of John and reflects the vision and purpose of all of our publications: to be an instrument of the Spirit, whose desire is to manifest Jesus' presence in and to the children of God. In this way, we hope to contribute to the Church's ongoing mission of proclaiming the gospel to the world so that all people would know the love and mercy of our Lord and grow more deeply in their faith as missionary disciples.

Our monthly devotional magazine, *The Word Among Us*, features meditations on the daily and Sunday Mass readings, and currently reaches more than one million Catholics in North America and another half million Catholics in one hundred countries around the world. Our book division, The Word Among Us Press, publishes numerous books, Bible studies, and pamphlets that help Catholics grow in their faith.

To learn more about who we are and what we publish, visit us at www.wau.org. There you will find a variety of Catholic resources that will help you grow in your faith.

Embrace His Word, Listen to God . . .

www.wau.org